THE LETHAL STRIKE

A Blueprint for 'Sovereign Nothing' and the Protocol of Kenosis

Laeticia Amaka Anene

THE LETHAL STRIKE

A Blueprint for 'Sovereign Nothing' and the
Protocol of Kenosis

Laeticia Amaka Anene

Prophetic Awareness & Healing Ministries (PAAHM)
P O Box 690042, Houston, 77269 Texas • USA

Published by:
Prophetic Awareness & Healing Ministries

P O Box 690042 Houston, Texas 77269, USA
www.paahm.org

Paperback ISBN: 979-8-9945883-1-4

Printed in the United States of America.

First Edition: March 2026

DEDICATION

*T*o the **Mercy of God Mission** and the rising army of leaders across the nations: May you have the courage to drop the crown, pick up the towel, and lead only as He leads.

To the **"Final Generation"**: Those who are tired of the architecture of ego and are longing for the authentic authority of the King. This blueprint is for you. The throne is already taken.

And to the people of **East and West Africa**: You are not merely a mission field; you are the heartbeat of the strike. This work is consecrated to the sanctity of the lives we serve.

FOREWORD

By Rev. Ebenezer O. Anene Jr.

I have had the distinct, often quiet privilege of watching the message of this book grow—not in a study or a library, but in the trenches of real life.

Many people write about leadership as a series of heights to be climbed. They speak of influence, reach, and the "Saul-like" stature that the world finds impressive. But as I have walked alongside the author, I have seen a different narrative unfold. I have seen the "Sovereign Nothing" that she writes about in these pages.
There is a weight to this book because it was born out of a refusal to bow to the systems of ego that dominate our modern institutions. In our travels, in our ministry, and in the private corners of our home, I have watched [Your Name] wrestle with the "whip and the towel." I have seen her stand with holy indignation against that which profanes the Father's house, only to turn around and wash the feet of those whom the world has overlooked.

The End of the Saul Regime is more than a title; it is a lifestyle I have witnessed firsthand.
To the reader: Do not approach this book as a casual observer. The "strike" the author describes is necessary for the health of the Church and the soul of the leader. I have seen the fruit of this message in her life, and I am confident that as you read, the Holy Spirit will begin the work of demolition in your own heart to make room for the true King.
The throne is indeed taken. It is my honor to introduce you to a blueprint that reminds us how to live like it.

Rev. Ebenezer O. Anene Jr. *Snr. Pastor*
Prophetic Awareness & Healing Ministries (PAAHM)

ACKNOWLEDGEMENTS

The life lived in the company of those who understand the cost of his work is not the product of a solo effort, but the result of a the "Whip" and the beauty of the "Towel."

To my husband, Ebenezer Obiora Anene: You are my primary example of the Sovereign Strike in action. Your strength, unwavering support, and partnership have been the bedrock upon which these words were written. Thank you for holding the space for me to find the "Nothingness" required to hear the King's voice. This book is as much yours as it is mine.

To my mother, Mrs. Gladys N. Egwuonwu: You set me on this path. Your influence on my life is the "Hidden Architecture" that gave me the structural integrity to stand. Your prayers and your example of faithfulness are woven into every chapter of this manuscript.

To my Children: You are my greatest motivation for ensuring that the next generation does not inherit a "Saul Regime." I write this so that you may see what true, Christ-like authority looks like—not as a burden of control, but as a mantle of protection.

Global Appreciation: I wish to extend my deepest gratitude to the global community of reformers, theologians, and "Sovereign Nothings" who are currently laboring in the wilderness to restore the Church and the marketplace. To every leader who has chosen the basin over the platform: this work is for you. We stand together in the Cloud of Witnesses.

THE SOVEREIGN MANUSCRIPT AUDIT

Core Objective: To dismantle the "Saul Regime" and equip "Sovereign Nothings" with the Lion-Lamb Symmetry.

The Structural Integrity Check

1. **The Spine (Theology):** You have moved from *Kenosis* (emptying) to *Tamiym* (wholeness). The theological thread is unbroken.

2. **The Muscle (Case Studies):** You have three high-density narratives (Logistics, Church Plant, Count Zinzendorf) that provide "Social Proof."

3. **The Nervous System (The 40-Day Fast):** You have a dayby-day practical application that prevents the book from being "theory-only."

4. **The Lethal Edge (The Glossary):** You have defined the "Language of the Strike," which creates a unique culture for your readers.

TABLE OF CONTENTS

EXECUTIVE SUMMARY

THE SOVEREIGN FRAMEWORK

To the Mission Leader, Executive, and Medical Director:

Their hands and the weight of a mission on their hearts. This book is written for those who carry the weight of lives in While the chapters follow a narrative journey of spiritual discovery, the ultimate goal is the transformation of your leadership culture.

To that end, this manuscript includes a formal **Seminary & Leadership Toolkit** located in the Appendix. This toolkit is specifically designed for:

- **Leadership Cohorts:** To be used as a four-week deep dive for your executive team.
- **Elder Boards:** To facilitate prayerful auditing of your ministry's health.
- **Succession Planning:** To help you identify and empower the "Agrammatos"—the unpolished but spiritually bold catalysts in your periphery.

The framework presented here—anchored in the principles of **Kenosis** (Self-Emptying), **The Braid** (Premeditated Discipline), and the **Cruciform Exit**—is not merely a philosophy. it is an invitation to move away from the "Palace of Saul" and into a leadership model that reflects the authority of Christ.

How to Navigate This Book:

- **For Personal Study:** Read chronologically to absorb the theological roots of these principles.
- **For Team Transformation:** Turn immediately to the **Sovereign Dialogue Guide** in the Appendix to begin a structured cohort session with your leadership team.

The health of a leader is not measured by their indispensability, but by the health of the organization after they depart.

PART I
THE ONTOLOGICAL SHIFT
(IDENTITY)

INTRODUCTION

DECONSTRUCTING THE SAUL REGIME

The Crisis of Fullness

We are currently witnessing the collapse of the "Saul Regime" in leadership. Across the global landscape—from the pulpits of mega-churches to the corner offices of Fortune 500 companies—the model of the "Large Leader" is breaking. We have been trained to lead through **Fullness**: full calendars, full bank accounts, full platforms, and full egos. We have equated "Presence" with "Noise" and "Authority" with "Visibility."

But the Saul model has a terminal flaw: it is **Image-Dependent. The Saul Archetype**

King Saul is the patron saint of the modern executive. He was chosen because he was "head and shoulders above the rest." He looked the part. He had the "Executive Presence" that the crowd demanded. However, Saul's leadership was a **Paywall.** He stood between the people and the Presence of God, using his position to curate an image rather than to facilitate a move of the Spirit.

The Saul Regime is characterized by:

1. **Fragile Identity:** Leading from a need for approval rather than a mandate of heaven.

2. **Defensive Competence:** Using power to protect one's position rather than to empower the "Nobodies."

3. **The Monument Trap:** Building structures that glorify the leader's name while the internal DNA of the organization rots.

When Saul felt the "Vacuum" of God's silence, he didn't wait in the nothingness; he forced the sacrifice. He chose **Fullness** over **Obedience**, and in doing so, he lost the Kingdom.

The Davidic Pivot: The Sovereign Nothing

In contrast stands the "Sovereign Strike" of the Davidic model—not the David of the throne, but the David of the **Wilderness.** The "Lethal Strike" does not come from the King's palace; it comes from the shepherd's sling. It is the authority of the leader who has become a **"Sovereign Nothing."** This leader has no reputation to protect, no brand to curate, and no ego to feed. Because they are empty of "Self," they can be filled with a "Weight of Glory" that the Saul Regime cannot comprehend.

The Anatomy of the Book

This is not a book about "Self-Improvement." It is a book about **Self Emptying.** Over the following chapters, we will deconstruct the four pillars of the Saul Regime and replace them with the **4 Cs of Sovereign Competence**:

- **Character:** Moving from Image to *Tamiym* (Wholeness).

- **Competence:** Mastering the Symmetry of the Lion and the Lamb.

- **Calling:** Shifting from Mentorship to DNA Transfusion.

- **Commitment:** Designing an Exit that honors the Cloud of Witnesses.

The Warning

To read this book is to invite a **Surgical Strike** against your own ambition. If you are looking for a way to grow your platform, put this book down. But if you are ready to "Clear the Room" so the King can enter—if you are ready to trade the "Crowd of the Present" for the "Cloud of Witnesses"—then you are ready for the Sovereign Strike.

It is time to flip the tables.

A Legacy of Friction

A Note from the Author
(The "Who"—Your personal experience)

Leadership is often sold as a seat at the table, but my journey has taught me it is more often a walk in the wilderness.

In these pages, I am not sharing theories polished in a classroom. I am sharing fire-tested truths forged in the silence of the mission field. I know the weight of leading three independent ministries while carrying the singular burden of a vision no one else could see. I have felt the "**Executive Solitude**" that comes when those you trust are blinded by the gold in your hand, while you are focused on the God who sent you.

I have stood in the gap during medical missions and healing conferences where the lack of transparency from my own team was more exhausting than the work itself. Yet, it was in those moments of total depletion—when the money was "little" and the zeal of others was gone—that I witnessed the **Divine Multiplier.** I have seen God take the fragments of my obedience and deliver undeniable miracles and global-scale outcomes.

If you have ever felt the sting of betrayal or the exhaustion of carrying a divine weight alone, let this be your evidence: **God comes through.** We aren't just leading; we are striking. And we are doing it from the only place of true authority: **The Cross.**

Laeticia Amaka Anene

CHAPTER 1

THE KENOSIS PROTOCOL

The Architecture of the Empty Seat

THE SAUL DIAGNOSTIC

Most leaders do not lose their way in a single, catastrophic moment of rebellion; they lose it in a thousand small compromises of convenience. We have become experts at building altars to our own influence while using the name of the King to decorate the lobby. This is the hallmark of the 'Saul Regime': an architecture that looks magnificent from the outside but is hollowed out by the rot of insecurity on the inside. Before you can THE LETHAL STRIKE, you must first have the courage to ask a terrifying question: **Are you building a Kingdom, or are you just building a monument to a man who is afraid of being forgotten?**

I. The Crisis of the "Full" Leader

Modern leadership—even within the hallowed halls of the seminary—is suffering from a famine of identity. We have mastered the art of "Self-Actualization," a psychological framework that tells the leader their success is found in becoming the most "maximized" version of themselves. We are told to "lean in," to "take up space," and to "project power." This is the **Shadow of Saul**.

King Saul was the perfect candidate on paper. He was "a head taller than any of the others" (1 Samuel 9:2). He was impressive, gifted, and chosen. But Saul led from a position of **Fullness**. His heart was full of his own reputation, his own fear of the people, and his own need to be seen as the source of victory. When a leader is "full" of themselves, they become a ceiling for the Holy Spirit. In the Kingdom, a "CEO Pastor" who manages a brand but doesn't know the soul of the sheep is not just a mismanagement—it is a structural failure of the highest order.

II. The Physics of the Kingdom Vacuum

To reconstruct the Christ-model, we must perform a surgical excavation of the **Kenosis Hymn** (Philippians 2:5-11). The Greek word kenos literally means "to be empty" or "to be void of content."

"Who, being in very nature God... made himself nothing."
(Philippians 2:6-7)

This is the **Architecture of the Empty Seat**. Most leadership books are about expansion; they teach you how to take up more space in the room. Christological leadership is about subtraction.

In physical science, a vacuum is a space devoid of matter. Nature abhors a vacuum; it will always rush to fill it. Spiritual leadership operates on the same law. When a leader refuses to fill a space with their own ego, their own cleverness, or their own "Brand," it creates a holy suction. When you make yourself "Nothing," you stop being a "Paywall" to the Presence and start being a "Conduit" for the Strike.

III. The Parable of the Glass Office Consider a leader named Samuel. He was a strategic genius who had built a magnificent organization. His office sat at the very top of his headquarters, encased in glass. He believed that for the mission to succeed, he had to be **Full**. He was the first to speak in every meeting and the final filter for every decision. He thought he was protecting the mission, but he was actually suffocating it. His team had become passive; they stopped bringing ideas because Samuel's "fullness" left no room for their contribution.

One Tuesday, a major logistics crisis threatened to shut down their operations. Samuel walked into the boardroom to "fill it." He spoke for forty minutes, asserting his authority and demanding answers. But the room remained cold. The problem didn't move.

That night, exhausted, Samuel encountered the **Kenosis Protocol**. He realized that by being the "Everything" of the organization, he had made God the "Nothing." The next morning, he called a meeting, sat at the end of the table, and said: *"I have no answers. I am emptying myself of the need to be the smartest person in this room. What does the Spirit say to you?"*

For ten minutes, there was a **Vacuum**. It was uncomfortable. But then, a junior staff member who had been silent for two years spoke up with a solution so precise it could only have been divine. Because Samuel made himself "Nothing," the "Everything" of God's wisdom finally had a place to land.

IV. The Linguistic Weapon: Doulos vs. Arche

In the corporate boardroom, "emptying yourself" sounds like a recipe for a coup. We argue the absolute opposite: The leader who operates as a **"Sovereign Nothing"** becomes an unshakeable conduit for the mission.

1. **The Arche:** Most leaders are obsessed with their *Arche*—their right to rule, their title, and their position. They lead from the "Top-Down."

2. **The Doulos:** The Kenosis Protocol demands a shift toward the identity of the *Doulos* (the Bondservant). A *Doulos* has no legal right to their own time, reputation, or output.

When you lead as a bondservant, you become **Un-offendable**. You cannot insult a man who has already died to his reputation. You cannot threaten a leader who owns nothing. This "Nothingness" is your greatest protection and your most lethal weapon.

V. The Mechanics of Emptying

How do we practice the Kenosis Protocol in the boardroom or the sanctuary?

1. **Selective Silence:** Choosing not to speak first. Let the "Money Changers" reveal their hearts in the silence you create.

2. **Reputation Fasting:** Refusing to correct every misunderstanding. Let the Cloud of Witnesses be your defense.

3. **The Lower Seat:** Intentionally taking the position of least honor to see who in your organization is chasing the "Pedestal."

VI. The Strike Action: Institutional Lab

A leader who cannot be honest with themselves can never be trusted with the souls of others.

- **The Source of Joy:** If your title, platform, and public recognition were stripped away tonight, what would remain of your joy? If the answer is "nothing," you are currently leading a Saul Regime.

- **The Shadow:** What is the one thing in your organization that you are most afraid for people to find out? Saul's downfall began with a secret sacrifice; yours will begin with a secret insecurity.

Practicum: The "Last Word" Fast

The Strike: In every meeting this week, you are forbidden from having the last word. You may provide the vision, but you must allow your team to offer the final clarification.

The Audit: If you feel the itch to "re-assert" your dominance at the end of a conversation, you have identified where your ego still sits on the throne.

CHAPTER 2

HOLY FRICTION

Dismantling the Architecture of Ego

> **"Holy Friction is the sound of the old regime giving way to the new mandate. Do not fear the sparks; fear the silence of a room that has stopped caring about the truth. If you are not willing to endure the friction of the Truth, you will never enjoy the fire of the Spirit."**

We have been conditioned to believe that peace is the absence of conflict. In the Saul Regime, 'peace' is often just a code word for silence, compliance, and the avoidance of truth. But the leadership of Christ introduces a different element: Holy Friction. It is the grit that occurs when the holiness of God rubs against the jagged edges of human ego. It is the heat generated when truth meets a lie. If your leadership has no friction, it likely has no movement. To THE LETHAL STRIKE is to understand that the whip in the temple was not an act of uncontrolled anger, but an act of Holy Friction—a divine disruption intended to clear the room so that the house could once again become a place of prayer.

The Lamb with a Whip: Tactical Disruption

Theological Thesis: Service is not passivity, and humility is not weakness. True Christ-centered competence requires the "Symmetry of Authority"—the ability to wash feet and flip tables in the same hour.

I. The Myth of the Passive Leader

We have been conditioned to believe that "peace" is the absence of conflict. In the Saul Regime, peace is often just a code word for silence, compliance, and the avoidance of truth. This is the **Architecture of Ego**—a towering structure of human charisma that looks like the Kingdom but lacks the King.

In these systems, "Servant Leadership" has been neutered into a brand of perpetual niceness. We have been taught that to THE LETHAL STRIKE is to be a passive enabler. **This is a theological lie.** If your leadership only includes washing feet and never flipping tables, you are merely managing a status quo. You are a "Lamb" without a "Lion," resulting in a leadership that is easily trampled. You have become an "enabler" of mediocrity rather than a "steward" of holiness. Like Saul, you may be "a head taller" than the rest, but you are hollow. Many leaders today follow this "Saul-style" growth, building systems that are held together by personality rather than Presence. In these systems, "Servant Leadership" has been neutered into a brand of perpetual niceness.

We have been taught that to THE LETHAL STRIKE is to be a passive enabler. This is a theological lie. If your leadership only includes washing feet and never flipping tables, you are merely managing a status quo. You are a "Lamb" without a "Lion," resulting in a leadership that is easily trampled.

II. The Lion-Lamb Paradox

True Christ-centered competence requires the **"Symmetry of Authority"**—the ability to wash feet and flip tables in the same hour. To THE LETHAL STRIKE, we must overcome the catastrophic "Spirit of Divorce" that separates the Lamb from the Lion:

1. **The Passive Lamb:** These leaders mistake "niceness" for holiness. They avoid conflict at all costs, allowing toxicity to fester. Under their watch, the "Money Changers" run rampant because no one is willing to flip the tables. This is **Institutional Cowardice**.

2. **The Carnal Lion:** These leaders lead through intimidation and raw power. They flip tables with a shotgun, not a braid. They destroy the "Sheep" along with the "Money Changers" because their friction is rooted in their own insecurity. This is **Tyranny**.

The **Sovereign Strike** only occurs when these two natures are perfectly fused. You must be a "Lamb" in your own identity—sacrificial and tender—but a "Lion" in your mission—lethal and unyielding.

III. The Raw Word: The Braid and the Strike

We must look at Jesus in the Temple (John 2:13-17) through the lens of **Executive Deliberation**. Jesus did not "lose His temper." This was not a tantrum; it was a calculated, surgical intervention.

- **The Braid (Preparation):** The text implies He sat down and made a whip of cords. This took time. The Lamb was braiding in the quiet, deliberate work of preparation.
- **The Strike (Execution):** The Lion was striking in the public, high-stakes execution of justice.

He targeted the **Infrastructures of Obstruction**—those who turned the "Court of the Gentiles" into a paywall for the elite. Your right to "Lion-like" disruption is mathematically proportional to your "Lamb-like" sacrifice. If you haven't washed the feet of those you lead, you have no moral authority to flip their tables.

IV. Case Study: The Logistics of the Spirit

I once observed an institutional system that was a perfect "Saul Regime." It had the most professional equipment, the best social media presence, and a perfectly polished leader. On paper, it was a success.

However, they had built a "Strange Altar" to efficiency. They spent 90% of their energy on the *logistics*—the flights, the funding, the scheduling—and only 10% on the *Life* of the Spirit. When a real crisis hit, the logistics could not save them. The architecture was magnificent, but it was hollow.

It wasn't until the leader introduced **Holy Friction**—refusing to look away from the structural flaws and "braiding a cord" of accountability—that the Life of the Spirit returned. They had to stop protecting the **Brand** and start protecting the **Body**.

V. The Stewardship of Friction

Friction is the grit that occurs when the holiness of God rubs against the jagged edges of human ego. Without friction, there is no traction. Without traction, there is no movement.

As a **Sovereign Nothing**, your "Roar" is never in defense of yourself. You have no reputation to protect. Therefore, when you strike, it is with clinical precision to protect the Sanctity of the Mission. You flip the table because the table is blocking the "Nobodies" from reaching the Presence.

VI. Strike Action: The Table-Flipping Audit

Answer these questions with lethal honesty to see if you are a Peacekeeper or a Peacemaker:

1. **The Price of Silence:** What is the true cost of the silence you are maintaining in your organization right now? Are you protecting the mission, or just your own comfort?

2. **The Money-Changer Audit:** Identify one "high-performer" on your team who is toxic—someone who hits their numbers but leaves a trail of broken spirits. Why haven't you flipped their table yet?

3. **The Heat Test:** If Christ walked into your boardroom today, what is the first table He would flip?

Practicum: Braid the Cord This week, identify one necessary confrontation. Spend 30 minutes in prayer "braiding the cord"— writing down exactly how this disruption serves the Mission and not your own frustration. Execute the strike only after the Lamb has finished the braiding.

IV. Institutional Lab: The Table-Flipping Audit

- ***The Analysis:*** *Identify one "Money Changer" in your organization—a person or process that is technically "productive" but spiritually or culturally toxic.*

- ***The Strategy:*** *How do you confront this without losing your "Lamb" heart?*

- ***The Practicum: Braid the Cord.*** *Spend 30 minutes in prayer writing down exactly how a necessary confrontation serves the **Mission** and not your own frustration.*

Closing the Gap

The "Lethal Strike" is the result of this symmetry. When the world sees the Lamb, they expect a doormat. When they encounter the Lion, they are blindsided. It is the **Symmetry of Authority** that clears the room. You do not need to shout to be a Lion; you only need to be **Whole.**

Practicum: The Money-Changer Audit

- The Strike: Identify one high-performer on your team who is "toxic"—someone who hits their numbers but leaves a trail of broken spirits.

- The Audit: Most leaders keep "Money Changers" because they like the revenue they bring. A Christ-leader removes them because they value the Presence of the mission more than the profit of the person.

The Strike Action: Holy Friction is not about being difficult; it is about being different. You cannot ignite a movement if you are constantly trying to smooth things over. Answer these questions to see if you are a "Peacekeeper" or a "Peacemaker":

1. **The Price of Silence:** Think of a specific conversation or decision in your organization right now that lacks "grit." What is the true cost of the silence you are maintaining? Are you protecting the mission, or are you just protecting your own comfort?

2. **The Heat Test:** When was the last time you stood your ground on a Kingdom principle and felt the "heat" of being misunderstood? If you cannot remember the last time you felt the sparks of Holy Friction, you may have unintentionally surrendered your mandate to the Saul Regime.

> **"If you are not willing to endure the friction of the Truth, you will never enjoy the fire of the Spirit."**

CHAPTER 3

THE RECRUITMENT PARADOX

The Saul Regime is obsessed with 'fit,' but the Sovereign Mandate is obsessed with 'Fruit.' Most leaders recruit for comfort; they surround themselves with mirrors that reflect their own insecurities and echoes that validate their own opinions. If your team only exists to serve your reputation, they will eventually become the weight that sinks your legacy. This is the Recruitment Paradox: the more you hire people 'just like you,' the less capacity you have to THE LETHAL STRIKE. Jesus did not recruit a fan club; He recruited a friction-point. He gathered a collection of misfits—tax collectors and zealots, fishermen and doubters—who had nothing in common except the call. To lead a strike against the status quo, you must stop looking for assistants who make your life easier and start looking for practitioners who make the mission sharper.

Choosing "Nobodies" to Lead a Revolution

Theological Thesis: The Kingdom of God bypasses the "Credentialed Elite" to find the "Calloused Available." Recruitment in the Christ-model is a paradox: God chooses the foolish things of the world to shame the wise.

I. The Failure of the Pedigree

The modern institutional model is obsessed with talent acquisition based on CVs, Ivy League degrees, and social status. We hire based on "Fullness"—we look for leaders who are already full of their own methods, pedigrees, and past successes. We scan for the "Best and the Brightest," believing that if we gather enough human light, we will eventually illuminate the world. But Jesus bypassed the Sanhedrin—the PhDs and religious executives of His day—and headed for the docks.

But the Kingdom operates on a **Recruitment Paradox**. God does not look for the "Full"; He looks for the **Empty**. He does not look for the "Bright"; He looks for the **Broken**. Why? Because a leader who is full of their own light has no room for the King's glory. A leader who is impressed by their own resume is a "Paywall" to the Presence. Jesus bypassed the Sanhedrin—the PhDs and religious executives of His day—and headed for the docks. He wasn't looking for the most "learned" (*grammatos*); He was looking for those who were "available" (*idios*). He looked for those who had the capacity to be "empty" enough to receive a new wineskin.

Why the King Chooses Nobodies

The Meritocracy of the World vs. The Mercy of the Strike

The Saul Regime is obsessed with "Elite Procurement." In the corporate and institutional world, we have been trained to scan for the "Full": full resumes, full pedigrees, and full charisma. We look for the "Best and the Brightest," believing that if we gather enough human light, we will eventually illuminate the world.

But the Kingdom operates on a **Recruitment Paradox.** God does not look for the "Full"; He looks for the **Empty.** He does not look for the "Bright"; He looks for the **Broken.** Why? Because a leader who is full of their own light has no room for the King's glory. A leader who is impressed by their own resume is a "Paywall" to the Presence.

The Sovereign Strike requires a specific kind of "Nothingness" in the hands of the recruit. If the tool thinks it is the craftsman, the work will be marred.

II. The Raw Word: Agrammatos vs. Arche

The Agrammatos Advantage

One of the most profound moments in the early church occurred in Acts 4:13: *"Now when they saw the boldness of Peter and John, and perceived that they were **uneducated and untrained men**, they marveled."*

The Greek word for "uneducated" is *agrammatos*—it literally means "unlettered" or "without credentials." To the Saul Regime, Peter and John were "Nobodies." They were the "unwashed" from the docks. Yet, they possessed a "Boldness" that silenced the Sanhedrin.

The **Agrammatos Advantage** is the authority that comes from **Selective Intimacy** with Christ rather than institutional validation. When a "Nobody" stands in the room, the world is forced to look past the person and see the Source. The recruitment of the "Nobody" is a strategic move to ensure that the "Excellence of the Power" belongs to God and not to men.

In Acts 4:13, the elite were astonished by Peter and John because they realized they were *agrammatos* (unlettered/common). But they also noted that "they had been with Jesus."

- **The Gethsemane Grit:** Jesus looked for callouses. Fishermen knew how to work through a cold, dark night without a catch and still have the strength to wash the nets the next morning. This is the grit required for long-term Kingdom work.

- **The Diversity of Friction:** Look at His recruitment strategy: He put a Zealot (a political revolutionary) and a Tax Collector (a Roman collaborator) in the same inner circle. He didn't want "Yes Men"; He wanted a collision of worldviews that could only be unified by the Mission.

III. The Callous Check: Scouting for Grit

How does a Sovereign Leader recruit? We do not look at the "Diploma"; we look at the **"Docks."** We look for **Callouses**. In the "Physics of the Kingdom," a callous is proof of *Hupomonē*—the power to remain under weight. A callous is a scar that has turned into armor.

- **The Gethsemane Grit:** Jesus looked for callouses. Fishermen knew how to work through a cold, dark night without a catch and still have the strength to wash the nets the next morning.

- **The Diversity of Friction:** Jesus put a Zealot (a political revolutionary) and a Tax Collector (a Roman collaborator) in the same inner circle. He didn't want "Yes Men"; He wanted a collision of worldviews that could only be unified by the Mission.

A "Polished" leader is often brittle; they break when the "Midnight Season" hits. But a "Calloused" leader has been through the fire. A gift can get you on a platform, but only grit can keep you in the Gethsemane moments of leadership.

IV. The Transfusion of the "Little Ones"

The Saul Regime recruits in the "Spotlight." The Sovereign Strike recruits in the **"Shadows."** Jesus did not recruit a "Dream Team"; He recruited a **"Death Team"**—men who were willing to die to their own ambitions because their previous ambitions had reached a dead end.

This is the **Transfusion of Identity**. Because these recruits had nothing to lose—no reputation, no brand, no status—they had everything to gain. The Sovereign Leader's greatest task is to find these "Little Ones" and transfuse the DNA of the King into them. You are looking for those who are empty enough to be filled and low enough to be lifted.

In the modern context, this means looking past the "Executive Spark" and searching for the **"Servant's Stain."** It is the intern who stays late to clean the breakroom without being asked; it is the junior manager who takes the blame for a team failure to protect their subordinates. These are the "Nobodies" who carry the "Somebody" named Jesus.

V. Institutional Lab: The Callous Check

Recruitment is not about filling a seat; it is about starting a transfusion.

- **The Identification:** Review your current leadership pipeline. How many of your rising stars have a history of "NetWashing" (hidden, unglamorous faithfulness)?

- **The Interview:** Stop asking about past successes. Ask: *"Tell me about a time you worked for a year on a project that failed, and you were the only one left to clean up the mess."* If they have no answer, they have no callouses.

- **The Selection:** Look at your current team. Are they "yes men," or are they "braided cords"?

Practicum:

> **The Hidden Transfusion Identify one "hidden" person in your organization who is working faithfully without recognition. Spend 15minutes today "transfusing" vision into them. Affirm their grit, not just their gift.**

VI. The Strike Action: The Echo Test

Look at your inner circle—the three to five people you rely on most. Answer these with Sovereign clarity:

1. **The Echo Test:** When was the last time someone on your team told you that you were wrong? If you can't remember, you haven't recruited a team; you've recruited an audience.

2. **The Competence Gap:** Are you afraid to hire someone who is smarter or more gifted than you in a specific area? If so, your "Saul" is showing.

3. **The Burden of Proof:** Are you recruiting based on a resume (The World's standard) or based on a "Cruciform" alignment (The Kingdom standard)?

Practicum: The Callous Check

- **The Strike:** Review your inner circle. Are they "Yes Men" who make you look great, or are they "Nobodies" who have a history of working through the night without a catch?

- **The Audit:** Stop looking at the CV. Ask your next potential hire: *"Tell me about a time you were hidden and unappreciated for a year, yet you still finished the task."* If they have no answer, they have no callouses.

The Strike Action: Look at your inner circle—the three to five people you rely on most. Answer these with Sovereign clarity:

1. **The Echo Test:** When was the last time someone on your team told you that you were wrong? If you can't remember, you haven't recruited a team; you've recruited an audience.

2. **The Competence Gap:** Are you afraid to hire someone who is smarter or more gifted than you in a specific area? If so, your "Saul" is showing.

3. **The Burden of Proof:** Are you recruiting based on a resume (The World's standard) or based on a "Crusiform" alignment (The Kingdom standard)?

> **"If your team only exists to serve your reputation, they will eventually become the weight that sinks your legacy."**

PART II
THE FIRST C – CHARACTER
(THE ARCHITECTURE)

CHAPTER 4

THE TAMIYM FACTOR

In the Saul Regime, character is treated like a costume—something you put on for the platform and take off in the private quarters. But the Sovereign Strike requires something deeper: Tamiym. In the ancient scripts, *Tamiym* isn't just 'good behavior'; it is the quality of an animal brought for sacrifice—it means without blemish, complete, and structurally whole. Most leaders are cracked vessels trying to hold holy water. They wonder why their influence leaks and their mandates fail. It is because they have substituted 'reputation' (what people see) for 'Tamiym' (who you are when the room is empty). You cannot lead a strike against a broken system if you are hiding a break within yourself. Character is the only floor that can support the weight of the King.

The Structural Myth of "Work-Life Balance"

The Saul Regime has popularized the myth of "Work-Life Balance," suggesting that a leader is a collection of separate compartments: the Professional, the Private, and the Spiritual. We are told we can have a "leak" in our private character as long as the "roof" of our public competence remains intact.

This is an architectural lie. In the Kingdom, integrity is defined as **Tamiym**—wholeness and undividedness. The Hebrew word refers to a sacrificial lamb "without blemish." It does not mean perfection; it means **Undividedness**.

If there is a "Gap" between who you are on the platform and who you are in the dark, you have a structural flaw in your foundation. When the "Weight of Glory" (the *Kabod*) eventually rests on your leadership, the structure will collapse—not because the weight was too heavy, but because the gap was too wide.

II. The Rebar of the Soul

In civil engineering, the strength of a skyscraper is not determined by the glass facade or the height of the spire; it is determined by the **rebar**—the hidden steel grid buried inside the concrete.

Leadership character is the rebar of the soul. We live in a "Facade Culture" where leaders are encouraged to polish their "Glass Exterior"—their charisma and social media presence. But when the "winds" of crisis or the "weight" of responsibility increase, the facade cannot save the building. **Tamiym is the rebar.** It is the internal consistency that allows a leader to withstand the "High Winds" of criticism and the "Earthquakes" of betrayal.

III. The Raw Word: The Integer of the Heart

The word "Integrity" comes from the Latin *integer*, meaning a whole number. An integer is not a fraction.

- **The Davidic Standard:** Psalm 78:72 tells us that David led them with "integrity of heart" and "skillful hands." Notice the order. The heart (*Tamiym*) preceded the hands (Competence).

- **The A-B-C of Authority:** Character is the "Root." If this is missing, the other three—Competence, Compassion, and Courage—become dangerous weapons of a carnal ego.

IV. The Shadow Economy: A Surgical Audit

Every leader has a "Shadow Economy"—the hidden motivations

and secret habits that drive their public performance. Saul's shadow economy was his **Need for Approval**. He traded his *Tamiym* for a Trend. To execute a Sovereign Strike, you must audit your own shadow:

1. **Linguistic Integrity:** Does your internal "Logos" match your external "Rhema"? Do you use spiritual language to hide carnal ambition?

2. **The Hidden Economy of Motive:** Are you washing feet because you want to be a servant, or because you want to be *seen* as a servant?

3. **The Consistency of the Basin:** Is your level of excellence the same when you are cleaning the "Basin" (the hidden task) as it is when you are holding the "Scepter" (the public task)?

V. Institutional Lab: The Structural Stress Test

You cannot flip a table of corruption if your own "hidden tables" are cluttered with compromise.

- **The Hidden Audit:** Identify one secret habit, thought pattern, or financial practice that you hope your team never discovers.

- **The Alignment:** Why does that secret exist? Is it a "rusted" piece of rebar in your soul?

- **The Confessional Peer:** Identify one "Nathan" in your life— a peer who is not impressed by your title. Give them full

- access to your "Hidden Room." If you have no one who can

- tell you "No," you are already in a state of structural collapse.

VI. Strike Action: Closing the Gap

The Sovereign Strike is only effective when it is launched from a "Whole" foundation.

1. **The Compartment Test:** Is there a part of your life—financial, relational, or digital—that you keep behind a locked door? If your leadership is compartmentalized, it is not *Tamiym*.

2. **The Weight Test:** As your influence grows, do you feel more pressure to "perform" or more freedom to "be"? A *Tamiym* leader is lighter because they have nothing to hide.

3. **The Altar Check:** Are you offering God your "best" publicly while giving Him your "leftovers" privately?

Practicum:
The Solitude Audit The Strike:
> **Spend 60 minutes in absolute silence—no phone, no Bible, no notebook, no worship music. Just you and the Creator. The Audit: Note the "noise" that rises in the silence. That noise is the sound of your "Self" protesting its own displacement.**

God does not use great men; He uses whole men. And He breaks the great ones until they are whole.

CHAPTER 5

KILLING THE IMAGE

The greatest enemy of Kingdom competence is the curated image. We have produced a generation of leaders who are world-class at the 'aesthetic' of authority but functionally illiterate in the 'execution' of the Spirit. Saul was a master of the image; he stood head and shoulders above the rest, looking every bit the king while losing the kingdom in real-time. To move into Sovereign Competence, you must first commit to Killing the Image. You must be willing to look unskilled to the world to remain sharp for the King. True competence isn't about how you appear on the platform; it is about the quiet, rigorous mastery of your craft when no one is watching. If your reputation is more developed than your actual ability, you aren't a leader—you are an actor.

I. The Idol of the Brand

We live in an era where "Personal Branding" is considered a professional necessity. We are told that our "reach" is our "value." Even in the Church, we have created a "Celebrity Industrial Complex" where leaders are managed like pop stars. We curate filters, edit captions, and measure "success" by the digital applause of people who do not know our names.

This is the primary rival to your Christ-Identity. You cannot lead a revolution while you are still checking your approval ratings.

To execute the Sovereign Strike, you must be willing to let your public "Image" die so that your spiritual "Identity" can live. A leader enslaved to the crowd is a leader who has already surrendered their sword. Saul was a master of the image; he stood head and shoulders above the rest, looking every bit the king while losing the kingdom in real-time.

II. The Raw Word: The Kenosis of Reputation

In Philippians 2, the **Kenosis Protocol** reveals that Christ *"made himself of no reputation."* In the Greek, this implies a voluntary emptying of status.

- **The Voluntary Misunderstanding:** Jesus was perfectly comfortable being misunderstood. He didn't send out a press release to clarify His comments to the Pharisees. He was so secure in His Identity as the Beloved Son that He was completely indifferent to His Image as the "Friend of Sinners."
- **Death Row for the Ego:** When you "Kill the Image," you lose the fear of being "canceled." You cannot cancel a dead man. A leader who has undergone the "Reputation Fast" is the only leader truly free to speak the truth, regardless of the cost.

III. Identity as Your Only Currency

If your identity is found in your "Performance," you will be a slave to your results. If your identity is found in your "Position," you will be a slave to your Board. But if your identity is found in your "Adoption," you become a Sovereign Leader. You lead from a position of Fullness in Christ rather than a position of Need for validation. Competence is a weapon, but it must be wielded by a hand that doesn't tremble for applause.

IV. Institutional Lab: The Image Deconstruction

True competence isn't about how you appear on the platform; it is about the quiet, rigorous mastery of your craft when no one is watching.

- **The Branding Audit:** Review your last three public engagements. How much of that content was designed to "Build the Mission" vs. "Build your Image"?

- **The "Unpopular" Strike:** Identify one decision you know God wants you to make, but you've been avoiding because it will "look bad" to your peers.

- **The Student Test:** Do you avoid tasks where you might look "unpolished"? If you are afraid to be a student, you have ceased to be a Sovereign Practitioner.

V. The Reputation Fast: The Nervous System Check

Observe the "twitch" to be right. If you cannot sleep until the record is set straight, your reputation has become your idol.

Practicum: The Reputation "Death Row" The Strike: For the next 30 days, do not "Google" yourself, do not check your "likes," and do not defend yourself against unfair criticism. **The Execution:** The next time you are misrepresented, do not send the "clarifying" email. Do not post the "rebuttal." Let God be your Vindicator. If you can stay silent, you have finally found the "Sovereign Nothing."

VI. The Strike Action: The Mirror vs. The Tool
Perform this final audit of your persona:

The Social Media Test: If you were forbidden from posting about your work for six months, would you still do it with the same level of excellence?

1. **The Feedback Loop:** Are you recruiting an audience to admire your image, or a team to execute the mission?
2. **The Final Verdict:** Is your competence designed to make you look good, or to make the mission succeed?

> **A leader who is obsessed with their shadow will eventually trip over their own feet. Kill the image, and let the work speak for the King."**

PART III
THE SECOND C – COMPETENCE
(THE TACTICAL EDGE)

CHAPTER 6

THE SYMMETRY OF AUTHORITY

In Sovereign Strike, competence is a Weaponized Stewardship. In the Saul Regime, competence is a performance; in the Most leaders fail not because they lack talent, but because their talent is not 'curded'—it hasn't been thickened by the fire of discipline or the weight of the Cross. Part III is where the 'Sovereign Nothing' begins to move. We are no longer discussing *who* you are; we are discussing *how* you strike. True competence is the ability to handle the Father's business with such precision that your own personality disappears into the excellence of the work. If you are still the most visible part of your success, you haven't mastered your craft—you've only mastered your stage presence. A leader who refuses to exit isn't just "present"—they have become a **"Carnal Lion"** protecting their territory.

I. The Tragedy of the Unbalanced Leader

Most leadership failures are failures of **Symmetry**. We have produced two types of casualties in the modern institution:

1. **The Tyrant (The Lion without the Lamb):** They hit KPIs and win market share but leave a trail of scorched earth. They

use people as "resources" rather than "sheep." They have power, but no Presence.

2. **The Enabler (The Lamb without the Lion):** They are "nice," but their organizations are chaotic. They allow toxicity to fester because they are too afraid to confront. They have presence, but no Power.

The Christ-leader rejects both. We look for the **Symmetry of the Scars.** In Revelation 5, John is told to look at the *Lion*, but when he turns, he sees a *Lamb*. Power is earned through sacrifice; authority is exercised through the "Wrath of the Lamb." Jesus was tender with the broken (The Lamb) but lethal toward the religious hypocrite (The Lion). He knew exactly which version of authority the moment required.

II. Professional Excellence as Worship

Competence is the stewardship of skill. A sloppy leader is a poor witness to a Sovereign God. We do not "wing it" on anointing; we work as unto the Lord.

- **The Skill of the Shepherd:** A shepherd must know how to use the "Staff" to guide and the "Rod" to protect. If the shepherd is incompetent with his tools, the sheep pay the price.

- **Arēte (Excellence):** The leader must be a craftsman of their craft—whether it is finance, design, or soul-care. We must be so excellent that the world cannot mock the Message because of the sloppiness of the Medium. Arēte is not just a high KPI; it is the moral excellence of a tool that does exactly what it was forged to do.

III. The Call to Action: Execute the Silence

A Saul Regime leaves a trail of **Noise**—it is loud, defensive, and demands to be acknowledged. But the Sovereign Strike leaves a trail of **Silence**. This is the silence of absolute alignment; the silence of a sharp blade through silk. Stop trying to prove your competence to the crowd. Go back to the grain of the wood. Sharpen your tools in the secret place until your execution is so undeniable that you no longer have to announce your arrival.

IV. Institutional Lab: The Symmetry Audit

Sloppy work is a form of spiritual arrogance.

- **The Self-Assessment:** On a scale of 1 to 10, are you a "Lion" (Confrontational) or a "Lamb" (Empathetic)?

- **The Re-Balance:** If you are a 9 Lion, wash the feet of someone you find difficult. If you are a 9 Lamb, issue a formal "Braid the Cord" correction this week.

- **The Excellence Check:** Identify one area of your leadership that is "sloppy" (punctuality, budget, follow-through). Fix it by Friday.

> **Practicum: The Lion/Lamb 360 The Strike: Ask your most honest team member: "Do I lean toward being a doormat or a dictator when the pressure is high?" The Execution: If the answer is "doormat," confront one area of mediocrity you've been ignoring. If "dictator," perform a task "beneath" your rank for a subordinate.**

V. The Strike Action: The Invisibility Factor

Competence is a weapon, but it must be wielded by a hand that doesn't tremble for applause.

1. **The Sharpness Test:** What is the one skill required for your mandate that you have neglected because you were too busy managing your image?

2. **The Stewardship Audit:** If God audited your current level of excellence, would He find a "sharp sword" or a "rusty blade"?

3. **The Result:** In your greatest achievement this year, did people marvel at *you*, or did they marvel at the *impact*?

4. **Explicitly state:** "If you cannot leave, you have stopped being a Shepherd and started being a Landlord."

Kingdom competence is the art of doing the work so well that God gets the credit and the enemy gets the headache.

PART III:
THE SECOND C – COMPETENCE (CONTINUED)

CHAPTER 7

BRAIDING THE CORD

Most leaders mistake a tantrum for a transition. They react to institutional rot with the heat of their own triggers, calling it 'zeal' when it is actually just an ego defending its own comfort. But the Sovereign Strike is never reactive; it is always Premeditated. Before Jesus flipped a single table, He sat in the silence of the temple courts and braided a cord. Every twist of that leather was an act of prayerful auditing. Every knot was a strategic decision. To THE LETHAL STRIKE is to move beyond the 'hot-headed' outburst and into the Calculated Strike. If you are still reacting in the moment, you are being led by your flesh. If you are braiding, you are being led by the Spirit.

Premeditated Discipline vs. Emotional Reaction

I. The Myth of the Spontaneous Leader

Many leaders spiritualize their lack of emotional control as "prophetic fire." In reality, an uncalculated reaction is usually the Ego defending its own image or comfort. Christological competence is different. It is composed and deliberate.

The time it takes to braid the cord is the time required for **Executive Deliberation**. If you cannot wait long enough to braid the tool, you do not have the authority to use it. If you are reacting in the moment, you are being led by your triggers. If you are braiding, you are being led by the Spirit.

II. The Raw Word: The Pause of Power

When Jesus entered the Temple, the atmosphere was chaotic, but His spirit was composed. The "Braid" is the ultimate symbol of Kingdom Strategy. John 2:15 provides a detail most leadership manuals overlook: *"And making a whip of cords, he drove them all out of the temple."* * **The Calculated Strike:** Jesus did not walk into the Temple and start swinging. He stopped. He observed. He gathered materials. Every twist of that leather was an act of prayerful auditing. Every knot was a strategic decision.

- **Targeting the Infrastructure:** Notice what Jesus hit. He overturned the tables and poured out the coins. He targeted the **Infrastructure of Greed**, not the humanity of the person. He identified the "Paywalls to the Presence" that prevented the "Nobodies" from reaching God.

- **The Braid as Processing:** You must be sharp enough to flip the "Table" of a toxic process without crushing the "Person" who was trapped behind it.

III. The Infrastructure of Integrity

Competence is the ability to build systems that protect the mission. Most leaders suffer from "People Problems" that are actually **System Failures**.

- **The Braiding Problem:** If a staff member is consistently toxic and there has been no confrontation, the failure is yours. You have failed to Braid the Cord of accountability.

- **The Clean Temple:** A leader's job is to ensure the organization remains a place of access. If bureaucracy, ego, or politics have set up shop in your lobby, your mission is being strangled. Braiding the cord is the highest form of love because it restores the sanctity of the house.

IV. Institutional Lab: The Money-Changer Audit

Excellence is not the absence of conflict; it is the presence of Righteous Friction.

- **Identify the Paywall:** Pinpoint one process, person, or tradition in your organization that makes it harder for people to experience the mission. What is blocking the "court of the Gentiles" in your house?

- **The 48-Hour Braid:** Spend the next 48 hours "braiding the cord." Do not react. Document the issue. Align it with the original mandate. Design the correction while your heart is cool and your mind is sharp.

- **The Surgical Flip:** Execute the removal of the paywall. Target the process, not the person's worth. Flip the table, but keep the soul.

V. The Strike Action: The Reaction Test

A whip without a braid is just noise. A strike without a pause is just violence.

1. **The Reaction Test:** When was the last time you "swung" at a problem before you "braided" the solution?

2. **The Infrastructure Test:** Are you attacking people because you are too lazy to fix the systems that are breaking them?

3. **The Access Test:** If the King walked into your office today, whose "table" would be the first to go? Why is it still standing?

4. **The Temple Clearing:** If Christ walked into your boardroom or your ministry today, what is the first table He would flip? Why haven't you flipped it yet?

A whip without a braid is just noise. A strike without a pause is just violence. Master the art of the deliberate cord.

PART IV:
THE THIRD C – CALLING (THE ALIGNMENT)

CHAPTER 8

VENTURE CAPITAL OF THE SOUL

You are not a leader until you have successfully 'infected' a core group with your DNA so deeply that your presence is no longer the primary driver of the mission. Most modern leadership is obsessed with Information Transfer—the cold exchange of data, tasks, and KPIs. But the Sovereign Strike requires Identity Transfusion. Jesus didn't just give His followers a syllabus; He gave them His life. He invested the 'Venture Capital' of His soul into a few 'Nobodies' so that the mission could survive His absence. If your leadership requires you to be in the room for it to function, you haven't built a movement; you've only built a monument to your own indispensability.

From "Mentoring" to "Transfusion" I.

The Failure of Modern Mentorship

We have replaced "Discipleship" with "Mentorship." Mentorship is a professional exchange of information—a transactional way to network or climb a ladder. Discipleship is a spiritual transfusion of life.

Most modern leaders manage "Staff," but Christ built **Sons**. If you are leading employees, you are a manager. If you are leading *Doulos* (Bondservants), you are an Apostle. If you are only giving your followers "Information," you are a teacher. In a Kingdom context, a "Teacher" is actually a high calling. If you are giving them "Tasks," you are a manager. But if you are giving them your *Psuche* (Life), you are a leader. We are not called to produce "mini-me" versions of our success; we are called to produce Sons and Daughters of the Mission.

II. The Raw Word: Selective Intimacy

This is a "Lethal Strike" to the modern egalitarian view of leadership. Jesus did not treat everyone equally. He practiced **Selective Intimacy**. He had the crowds, the seventy, the twelve, and the three.

- **The 80/20 Rule of the Kingdom:** Jesus spent the vast majority of His vulnerability and prayer with the Twelve. He realized that to reach the world, He had to deeply "infect" the few.

- **The Deep Water of Koinonia:** Calling is "caught" more than it is "taught." Jesus allowed the inner circle to see His hunger, His exhaustion, and His Gethsemane. He didn't just teach them how to lead; He showed them how to bleed.

III. Hiring for the Scars

Investing the "Venture Capital" of your soul is a high-risk venture. One of the Twelve was a traitor; another was a denier; all were doubters. You are not looking for the most polished resume; you are looking for those whose souls are ready for a transfusion.

The Christ-leader does not withhold the transfusion because of the fear of betrayal. We invest because the **Succession of the Kingdom** depends on the multiplication of our DNA into the next generation. You are looking for those who are willing to lose their lives to find them.

IV. Institutional Lab: The Investment Portfolio

Stop building the institution for a moment and start building the people.

- **The Calendar Audit:** Review your last 30 days. How much time was spent on "Task Management" versus "Life Transfusion"? If your schedule is 100% administrative, your calling is currently dormant.

- **The Identification of the Three:** Who are the people in your life who carry the weight of the future mission? If you cannot name them, you are a bottleneck to the Spirit.

- **The Deep-Water Hour:** This week, cancel one administrative task. Take one of your "Three" to a place of vulnerability. Share a "scar"—not a success story, but a wound that became a portal for grace.

V. The Strike Action: The DNA Test

If you are only giving them information, you are a **Lecturer**. If you are giving them your *Psuche* (Life/Soul), you are a **Father**." Using *Psuche* here (as in John 10:11 where the Good Shepherd lays down His *psuche*) perfectly anchors your "Transfusion" concept.

Kingdom succession is not the passing of a torch; it is the pouring of a life.

1. **The DNA Test:** If you disappeared tomorrow, would the mission continue with the same intensity? If the answer is no, you haven't led; you've only dominated.

2. **The Vulnerability Test:** Do those closest to you know your "Gethsemane," or only your "Transfiguration"?

3. **The Sonship Test:** Are you surrounded by people who work
    for you, or people who are becoming like the Christ in you?

Kingdom succession is not the passing of a torch; it is the pouring of
a life. Spend the capital of your soul wisely.

CHAPTER 9

THE CALLOUS CHECK

he world recruits based on 'Fullness'—pedigrees, polished resumes, and the curated elegance of past successes. But the

Kingdom recruits based on Scars. When Jesus walked the shores of Galilee, He wasn't looking for the 'learned' (*grammatos*) who were full of their own ideas; He was looking for men with salt in their wounds and callouses on their hands. He was looking for the Agrammatos Advantage—the raw power of the unpolished who have the grit to stay on the boat when the storm is rising and the nets are empty. If you hire for 'Fit,' you get a fan club. If you hire for 'Friction' and 'Grit,' you get an army.

Hiring for Grit and Spiritual Callouses over Credentials

I. The Credential Trap

Institutions often fail because they hire for "Polished Potential." They look for the highest GPA and the most "Executive" presence. But the Christ-leader looks for the history of the **Hidden Years**.

When you hire someone who is full of their own credentials, you have no room to put the Mission into them. The Kingdom seeks the "Empty" and the "Calloused." These are people who don't have a reputation to protect, which makes them the only ones truly free to follow a lethal call. God does not call the qualified; He qualifies the called by testing their grit in the "net-washing" seasons of life.

II. The Raw Word: Hupomonē (The Power to Remain)

The Greek word *Hupomonē* is often translated as "patience," but its true meaning is far more aggressive. It is the capacity to remain under a crushing weight without breaking.

- **The Net-Washing Test:** In Luke 5, the disciples were "washing their nets" after a night of catching nothing. This is the ultimate Callous Check. Anyone can lead when the nets are full. A Christ-leader is formed in the faithfulness of the "Nets" when the "Fish" are nowhere to be found.

- **Grit over Gift:** Talent will get you on the stage, but only *Hupomonē* will keep you in the Wilderness. A person with a true "Calling" has a history of hidden faithfulness. They have been "Net-Washers" for years before they were "Fishers of Men."

III. The Agrammatos Advantage

The religious elite of Jesus' day were "full" of their own learning (*grammatos*). The fishermen were "empty" (*idios*) and therefore teachable. They had the Grit of the Docks.

The Recruitment Paradox: If you want to build a movement that outlasts you, stop hiring for "Comfort" and start hiring for "Calloused Availability." You are looking for those who have been "Hidden" for ten years in obscurity and didn't complain. The unpolished have the grit to stay on the boat when the storm is rising and the nets are empty.

IV. Institutional Lab: The Callous Assessment

Stop asking, "What did you accomplish?" and start asking, "What did you survive?"

- **The Interview Pivot:** In your next recruitment cycle, ignore the pedigree. Ask this: *"Tell me about a season where God had you in the 'Obscurity of the Net-Washing.' Why didn't you quit?"*

- **The Hidden Talent Scout:** Look deep into the lowest levels of your organization for a "Net-Washer"—someone doing dirty work with a great attitude and zero recognition. Give them a seat at a high-level table this week and observe how they handle the weight.

- **The Grit Metric:** Identify the hardest, least glamorous job in your organization. Is your current leadership team willing to do it? If not, your Symmetry of Authority is off-balance.

V. The Strike Action: The Survival Metric

If they have no callouses, they will fold the moment the "Whip" is required.

1. **The Scar Test:** Can this candidate point to a season of unappreciated, hidden labor?

2. **The Teachability Audit:** Are they more proud of what they know or what they are willing to learn?

3. **The Survival Metric:** Does this person have the *Hupomonē* to remain under the weight of a mandate when the results aren't visible?

God does not call the qualified; He qualifies the called by testing their grit in the hidden years. Hire the net-washers.

PART V

THE FOURTH C – COMMITMENT

(THE LEGACY)

CHAPTER 10

THE CRUCIFORM EXIT

The ultimate test of Christ-like leadership is not how well the organization functions in your presence, but how explosively it expands in your absence. Most leaders are seduced by the Pathology of Presence—the lie that their charisma is the glue holding the mission together. But the Sovereign Servant has a different goal: Obsolescence. To THE LETHAL STRIKE is to move toward your own disappearance so that the mission is no longer dependent on a personality, but propelled by a shared DNA. The 'Exit' is the final, lethal move against your own ego. If the mission requires your constant touch to survive, you haven't built a movement; you've built a monument to a man who is afraid to be forgotten.

I. The Pathology of the Indispensable Leader

One of the most seductive lies in leadership is the belief that your charisma is the glue holding the mission together. We often spiritualize our "need to be involved" as stewardship, but in reality, it is a **Pathology of Presence**.

When a leader refuses to let go, they become the ceiling of the organization. They create a "Founder's Trap" where every decision and every crisis-intervention must pass through their hands. This creates a **Bottleneck Institution**. If the mission requires your presence to survive, it is a monument to you. The Christ-leader understands that their highest commitment is not to their Position, but to the **Perpetuation** of the mandate.

II. The Raw Word: Tetelestai (The Completed Work)

When Jesus cried, *"It is finished"* (*Tetelestai*), He wasn't just announcing the end of His pain; He was announcing the completion of a structural handoff.

- **The Strategic Departure:** Jesus made the most counterintuitive statement in leadership history: *"It is for your good that I am going away"* (John 16:7). He realized that His physical presence was a ceiling. As long as He was in the room, the disciples remained "consumers" of His power rather than "producers" of the Kingdom.

- **Removing the Ceiling:** The Cruciform Exit is the intentional death of the leader's role so that the "Body" can take its place. By leaving, Jesus forced the Twelve to step into an authority they would never have claimed while He was holding the keys.

III. Designing Obsolescence

A Christ-leader begins their first day on the job looking for their replacement. They do not hoard "Keys" of authority; they hand them out.

- **The Apostolic Metric:** You are not a leader until your subordinates can do your job better than you.

- **The Shadow of Saul:** Saul clung to the throne until it destroyed him. David, however, prepared the materials for a Temple he would never build and handed the blueprints to the next generation. David led from the future; Saul led from the fear of losing the present.

IV. Institutional Lab: The Succession Audit

Identify your "Idols of Control" and dismantle them before they dismantle your legacy.

- **The "Hit by a Bus" Test:** Imagine you are called away for three months starting tomorrow with zero communication. Write down exactly what would break in the first 48 hours. Those points of failure are your **Ego Anchors**.

- **Handing Over the Keys:** Identify the people who should be handling those "failure points." Give them the authority (and the right to fail) this week. If you cannot trust them with the keys, you haven't been leading; you've been hoarding.

- **The Silent Week:** For one full week, attend all your regular meetings but do not speak unless asked a direct question. Observe the vacuum. If your team struggles, you haven't trained them. If they thrive, you have successfully "emptied" the seat.

V. The Strike Action: The Tetelestai Metric

Die to your position so the mission can live.

1. **The Vacuum Test:** Does your team look to you for the answer, or do they look to the Mandate?

2. **The Succession Audit:** Is there someone currently in your "inner circle" who is 80% ready to replace you? If not, your "Transfusion" (Chapter 8) has failed.

3. **The Final Verdict:** Can you look at your current project and say, "It is finished," even if you aren't the one to cross the finish line?

Kingdom leadership is the only race where the winner is the one who hands the baton off the fastest. Die to your position so the mission can live.

CHAPTER 11

FAITHFULNESS THROUGH TRIALS AND SUCCESS

Commitment is not a feeling; it is a Sovereign Stay. It is the terrifying ability to remain under the weight of the assignment when the 'Hosannas' of the crowd turn into the 'Crucify Him' of the critics. Most leaders are merely 'Mountaintop Committed'—they are in love with the feeling of winning. But the Christ-leader is forged in the Garden of Gethsemane, where the cup is bitter, the friends are asleep, and the only audience is the Father. Your legacy is not recorded in the buildings you built, but in the DNA you transfused into the next generation while you were bleeding.

I. The Trap of the Mountaintop

It is easy to be committed when the ministry is growing, the budget is overflowing, and the crowd is cheering. But "Mountaintop Commitment" is often just masked narcissism—we are committed to the feeling of winning.

Most leaders spend the final third of their careers "maintaining" what they built in the first two-thirds. They become risk-averse, protective, and spiritually stagnant. But a Christ-leader never switches to maintenance mode. If you build a seminary but don't build "Sovereign Nothings," you have only built a museum. A legacy

is not a building with your name on it; it is a person with your
Character (*Tamiym*) in them.

II. The Raw Word: The Sovereign Stay

True authority is written in the scars of your commitment. When the
disciples saw the risen Christ, they recognized Him not by His face,
but by His wounds.

As established in our recruitment of the "Net-Washers," the key is
Hupomonē—the power to stay on the cross when you have the legal
right to come down. This is the **Midnight Strike** against the enemy.
He can handle your talent, but he cannot handle your endurance.
True commitment is when your private "Yes" to God remains
unchanged even when your public reward is "No." If you refuse to
quit, you become a structural problem for the kingdom of darkness.

III. The Integration: The 4 Cs Final Seal

The 4 Cs are not a menu; they are a System. To remove one is to
collapse the Strike:

1. **Character** without **Competence** is impotence.
2. **Competence** without **Character** is tyranny.
3. **Calling** without **Commitment** is a fantasy.
4. **Commitment** without **Calling** is burnout.

IV. Institutional Lab: The Legacy Blueprint

Do not wait for the end of your life to audit your legacy.
The Obituary Exercise: Write your "Leadership Obituary" from the
perspective of a subordinate you once corrected with the "Braid." What
do they say about your heart?

- **The DNA Check:** List your organization's top five values.
  Now, ask five random staff members to list them. If they don't
  match, the Identity Transfusion has failed.

- **The Sacrifice of Hiddenness:** Identify the area where you
  feel most unappreciated. Instead of seeking validation, offer
  that "hiddenness" as a sacrifice. Declare: *"Even if no one sees
  this, the task is finished."* This is the birth of Sovereign
  Authority.

V. The Strike Action: The Final Room Check

*You have the blueprint. You have the Raw Word. You have the Lethal
Strike.*

1. **The Endurance Test:** Are you holding the line because of
   the reward, or because of the Mandate?
2. **The Scar Audit:** Does your leadership carry the evidence of
   what you were willing to suffer for the mission?
3. **The Room Check:** Is the room cleared? Is the table flipped?
   Is the King's house restored?
4. Calling is the target; Commitment is the *Hupomonē* that stays
   in the fight until the target is destroyed.

Kingdom leadership is the only race where the winner is the one who
hands the baton off the fastest. Now, go and clear the room.

POSTSCRIPT

THE SOVEREIGN SEND-OFF

The Empty Room

The King is not looking for more "leaders." The world is already saturated with them—men and women who have mastered the art of the polish, the branding, and the institutional dance. The Saul Regime is crowded. But the courts of the Sovereign Strike are quiet.

You have the 4 Cs. You have the **Raw Word**. You have the **Surgical Trim**.

But information without execution is just another form of "Fullness." If you finish this book and simply feel "inspired," you have failed. The goal was never to educate your mind; it was to weaponize your spirit.

The mandate is simple:

- **Go to your "Secret Place"** and find your "Nothingness." Until you are a "Sovereign Nothing," you cannot be trusted with "Everything."

- **Braid the Cord.** Stop reacting to the rot. Sit in the silence until the strategy is sharp and the strike is premeditated.

- **Flip the Tables.** Identify the paywalls to the Presence in your organization and dismantle them with clinical precision. Target the systems, save the souls.

- **Execute your Obsolescence.** Pour your life into the "Three" until your presence is no longer required for the mission to explode.

When the work is done, the greatest evidence of your authority will not be your name on a building or a title on a door. It will be the **Silence of Alignment**. It will be a room that has been cleared of clutter, a mission that is propelled by DNA, and a King who is finally at home in His house.

The room is waiting. The cord is in your hands.

Execute the Strike.

CONCLUSION

THE COMMISSIONING

Title: Go and Clear the Room

You did not pick up this book to become a better manager. You picked it up because you sensed that the architecture of your leadership was leaning too heavily on the strength of your own name. As you step away from these pages and back into the theater of your calling, you will immediately feel the gravity of the 'Saul Regime.' The pressure to curate your image, to appease the board, and to protect your platform will be immense. Do not yield.

Remember the Sovereign Nothing. A leader who has nothing to lose is the only leader the enemy cannot handle. When you finally stop leading for the Crowd of the Present—with their fickle applause and digital mirrors—and start leading for the Cloud of Witnesses, you become un-buyable and un-cancelable.

The members of that Cloud—the Pauls, the Marys, the reformers, and the martyrs—cannot be impressed by your office furniture or your 'executive presence.' They only recognize two things: your scars and your faithfulness. The tables in your temple are waiting to be flipped. The feet in your lobby are waiting to be washed. The 'Nobodies' in your shadows are waiting to be transfused with your DNA.

Do not seek a throne; seek a towel. Do not protect your brand; protect the sheep. The Lethal Strike of the Kingdom is not an act of violence, but an act of Sovereign Love—the courage to be 'Nothing' so that God can be everything. Your lap in the relay is half-finished. The baton is in your hand. The Cloud is watching."

THE FINAL PIVOT: FROM THE CROWD TO THE CLOUD
In the "Lethal Strike" framework, the Cloud of Witnesses (Hebrews 12:1) is the ultimate antidote to the Idol of the Audience. Most leaders are paralyzed by the 'Crowd of the Present'—the critics, the board, and the followers. When you lead for the Crowd, you are a performer. When you lead for the Cloud, you are a Sovereign.

1.   **The Death of the Digital Mirror: Killing the Personal Brand** The Cloud of Witnesses is the cure for the narcissism of the 'Personal Brand.' The saints who have finished the race through fire and blood are not moved by your social media following or your 'executive presence.' They see the moments you chose the 'Nothing' over the 'Something.' By shifting your focus to the silent approval of the saints, you empty yourself of the toxic need for earthly validation.

2.   **The Sanctification of the Secret: Validating the Hidden Years** Nothing is ever actually hidden. The 'Net-Washing'—the monotonous, unglamorous work in the shadows—is what the Cloud cheers for. This perspective provides you with Gethsemane Grit. You aren't working for a crowd that forgets; you are working for a Cloud that remembers. Your integrity in the secret place is your greatest strike in the public square.

3.   **Relinquishing the Baton: Preparing the Cruciform Exit** If you lead for the people in the room, you become a prisoner of the

room. You fear leaving because your identity is tied to the throne (The Founder's Trap). But the Cloud reminds you that you are merely one runner in a multi-generational relay. The Cloud is filled with those who had the courage to say, 'It is finished,' and step aside. You do not fear the Exit; you embrace it as the moment you finally join the Cloud yourself.

THE FINAL CHARGE

The world is looking for 'Somebodies.' The Kingdom is looking for 'Nobodies' who know a 'Somebody' named Jesus.

Do not protect your brand; protect the sheep.

Do not build a platform; build a basin.

Do not seek a throne; seek a towel.

The Lethal Strike is the courage to be the only person in the room willing to be 'Nothing' so that God can be 'Everything.' As you walk back into your temple, remember: the tables are waiting, the feet are waiting, and the Cloud is waiting for you to finish your lap.

Go and perform the Lethal Strike of the Kingdom. THE LETHAL STRIKE, until He is all in all.

THE APPENDICES
THE INSTITUTIONAL TOOLKIT

APPENDIX A

THE 12-WEEK SYLLABUS

COURSE TITLE: THE SOVEREIGN STRIKE
MASTERING THE 4 CS OF LEADERSHIP

Course Description: An intensive, ontological journey into the heart of Christological leadership. This course is designed to deconstruct the "CEO Mindset" and reconstruct the leader as a "Sovereign Nothing." Students will engage in weekly "Lethal Strike" Practicums to align their character, competence, calling, and commitment with the Kenotic pattern of Jesus.

WEEK 1: THE CRISIS OF FULLNESS (Chapter 1)

- **Reading:** Chapter 1: The Vacuum of Power.

- **The Lecture:** Examining the "Shadow of Saul" vs. the "Wait of David." Understanding how institutional success often masks spiritual bankruptcy.

- **The Lab:** *The Indispensability Audit.* Students must identify three organizational processes that would fail without them and design a "Vulnerability Plan" for each.

WEEK 2: THE KENOSIS PROTOCOL (Chapter 1)

- **Reading:** Philippians 2:5-11 (Greek Exegesis).

- **The Lecture:** *Doulos* vs. *Arche*. The physics of the Kingdom vacuum. Why the "leader with no reputation" is the only one who can carry true power.

- **The Practicum:** *The Last Word Fast.*

WEEK 3: THE SYMMETRY OF THE SCARS (Chapter 2)

- **Reading:** Chapter 2: Holy Friction.

- **The Lecture:** The Lamb-Lion Paradox. Analyzing the "Wrath of the Lamb" in the context of organizational health.

- **The Lab:** *The Table-Flipping Simulation.* Students will roleplay a confrontation with a "High-Performing Toxic Employee."

WEEK 4: BRAIDING THE CORD (Chapter 7)

- **Reading:** John 2:13-17.

- **The Lecture:** Premeditated Discipline. The difference between carnal anger and redemptive zeal. The theology of "The Braid."

- **The Practicum:** *The 48-Hour Processing Rule.*

WEEK 5: THE TAMIYM FACTOR (Chapter 4)

- **Reading:** Chapter 4: Integrity as Architecture.

- **The Lecture:** *Tamiym* (Wholeness) and the Integer of the Heart. The "Gap Theory" between platform and prayer closet.

- **The Lab:** *The Shadow Audit.* A guided, silent reflection on the "unseen" habits of the leader.

WEEK 6: MID-TERM REVIEW: THE REPUTATION FAST (Chapter 5)

- **Reading:** Galatians 2:20.

- **The Lecture:** The Death of the Image. Why "Personal

- Branding" is the enemy of Apostolic Authority.

- **The Practicum:** *30 Days of Zero Self-Defense.*

WEEK 7: TACTICAL EXCELLENCE (Chapter 6)

- **Reading:** Psalm 78:72.

- **The Lecture:** Competence as Worship. The stewardship of skill. Why "sloppy" leadership is a theological scandal.

- **The Lab:** *The Craftsmanship Audit.* Students identify one "mediocre" skill set and create a 90-day mastery plan.

WEEK 8: RECRUITING THE NOBODIES (Chapter 3)

- **Reading:** Chapter 3: The Recruitment Paradox.

- **The Lecture:** *Agrammatos* (The Unlettered) and the Gift of Obscurity. Why God chooses the "dock" over the "Sanhedrin."

- **The Practicum:** *The Callous Check Interview.*

WEEK 9: VENTURE CAPITAL OF THE SOUL (Chapter 8)

- **Reading:** Chapter 8: Transfusion.

- **The Lecture:** Selective Intimacy. The 80/20 rule of the Twelve and the Three. Moving from "Information" to "DNA Transfusion."

- **The Lab:** *The Calendar Realignment.* Moving from Task Management to Life-Transfusion.

WEEK 10: DISCERNING THE BURDEN (Chapter 9)

- **Reading:** Chapter 9: The Callous Check.

- **The Lecture:** Calling vs. Career. The theology of the "Burden" (Massa). Finding the "Sweet Spot" of Sovereign Alignment.

- **The Practicum:** *The Gethsemane Grit Test.*

WEEK 11: THE CRUCIFORM EXIT (Chapter 10)

- **Reading:** Chapter 10: The Theology of "It Is Finished."

- **The Lecture:** Designing Obsolescence. Why a leader's greatest success is their own replacement.

- **The Lab:** *The Succession Blueprint.* Draft a 12-month plan for handing over your current authority.

WEEK 12: FINAL COMMISSIONING (Chapter 11)

- **Reading:** Chapter 11: The Sovereign Legacy.

- **The Lecture:** The Cloud of Witnesses. The final 4 Cs integration.

- **Final Project:** Submission of the "Lethal Strike" Leadership Rubric (Appendix B).

APPENDIX B

THE 4 CS FORMATION RUBRIC

THE SOVEREIGN STRIKE DIAGNOSTIC TOOL

This rubric is designed for **Self-Audit** and **Peer-Evaluation**. It measures the leader's alignment across the four dimensions of the Sovereign Strike.

DIMENSION 1: CHARACTER (THE INTERNAL ARCHITECTURE)

- **Level 1 (The Shadow of Saul):** Integrity is situational. Significant "Gap" between public and private life. Driven by reputation and image management.

- **Level 3 (The Emerging David):** Aware of the "Gap." Engages in regular confession and solitude. Character is becoming the primary driver.

- **Level 5 (The Sovereign Nothing):** Private life is larger than public platform. No reputation to defend. Integrity is structural and unshakeable.

DIMENSION 2: COMPETENCE (THE TACTICAL SYMMETRY)

- **Level 1 (The Unbalanced):** Either a "Tyrant" (All Lion) or an "Enabler" (All Lamb). Sloppy execution and poor stewardship of skill.

- **Level 3 (The Braider):** Developing the ability to "Braid the Cord." Competence is seen as stewardship. Balancing empathy with discipline.

- **Level 5 (The Lion-Lamb):** Masters of the "Surgical Strike." Tactical excellence is used for the sanctity of the mission. Power is rooted in sacrifice.

DIMENSION 3: CALLING (THE STRATEGIC ALIGNMENT)

- **Level 1 (The Mercenary):** Leading for a paycheck or a title. Recruits for "Polished Potential." Focused on short-term tasks.

- **Level 3 (The Mentor):** Realizes the need for discipleship. Investing in a few "Nobodies." Calling is prioritized over career.

- **Level 5 (The Transfuser):** Successfully "infected" others with the mission DNA. Leading from a deep "Burden." Recruiting for callouses and grit.

DIMENSION 4: COMMITMENT (THE CRUCIFORM LEGACY)

- **Level 1 (The Bottleneck):** Clinging to authority. The organization collapses without their presence. Success is measured by personal visibility.

- **Level 3 (The Successor):** Actively training a replacement. Willing to be misunderstood for the sake of the future.

- **Level 5 (The Finisher):** Has successfully exited a previous role with an increase in mission impact. Success is measured by their obsolescence.

APPENDIX C

THE SOVEREIGN STRIKE FORMATION RUBRIC

Formation Clinical Diagnostic Tool for Spiritual &
Executive

A **Purpose:** This rubric serves as the primary assessment tool for the "Lethal Strike" Leadership track. It is designed to measure the integration of the 4 Cs (Character, Competence, Calling, Commitment) through the lens of **Lion-Lamb Symmetry**.

MODULE 1: THE CHARACTER AXIS (Tamiym Integrity)

Theological Goal: To move the student from "Performative Holiness" to "Structural Wholeness."

Section A: The "Gap" Analysis

- **Marker 1: Linguistic Integrity.** Does the student's private vocabulary match their public rhetoric? Do they use "spiritual language" to mask executive incompetence?

- **Marker 2: The Reputation Fast.** Can the student endure a 48-hour period of being "wrongly accused" without a carnal defense?

    - **Grading Matrix:**
        Level 1 (The Actor): High polish, low transparency.

- o Prone to image management.

  - o **Level 3 (The Transparent):** Honest about struggles but still seeks "human approval" as a primary motivator.

  - o **Level 5 (The Integer):** Operates as a "Sovereign Nothing." Identity is unshakeable regardless of public opinion.

MODULE 2: THE COMPETENCE AXIS (Lion-Lamb Symmetry)

Theological Goal: To produce a leader who can "Wash Feet and Braid Cords" with equal spiritual intensity.

Section B: Tactical Friction Management

- **Marker 1: The Braid Precision.** Can the student identify "Money Changers" in a simulated organizational environment? Is the intervention surgical (targeting the system) or carnal (targeting the person)?

- **Marker 2: The Basin & Towel Baseline.** Does the student possess the "Grit" to perform menial tasks (Net-Washing) when no "Cloud" or "Crowd" is watching?

- **Grading Matrix:**

  - o **Level 1 (The Dictator/Doormat):** Uses power to intimidate OR uses "niceness" to avoid responsibility.

  - o **Level 3 (The Emerging Shepherd):** Competent in tasks, but struggles with the emotional weight of "Holy Friction."

- o **Level 5 (The Sovereign Servant):** Masters the symmetry of authority. Uses the "Whip" to protect the Mission and the "Towel" to restore the People.

MODULE 3: THE CALLING AXIS (Transfusion Mechanics)

Theological Goal: To shift the focus from "Personal Career" to "Succession DNA."

Section C: The Agrammatos Recruitment

- **Marker 1: Grit Perception.** Can the student identify "callouses" in others, or are they only attracted to "polished credentials"?

- **Marker 2: The Selective Intimacy Protocol.** Does the student demonstrate the ability to invest 80% of their soul into a "Core Three"?

- **Grading Matrix:**

  - o **Level 1 (The Soloist):** Leads alone. Does not trust others with high-stakes tasks.

  - o **Level 3 (The Mentor):** Teaches others but does not "transfuse" life. Relationship is transactional.

  - o **Level 5 (The Apostle):** Lives for the success of the "Nobodies." Their primary joy is seeing their subordinates surpass them.

MODULE 4: THE COMMITMENT AXIS (Cruciform Legacy)

Theological Goal: To prepare the leader for a "Tetelestai" (It Is Finished) exit.

Section D: Obsolescence Design

- **Marker 1: The Succession Mindset.** Has the student documented their "Intellectual Capital" so it can be handed to a successor tomorrow?

- **Marker 2: The Cloud-Gaze.** Does the student demonstrate "Hupomonē" (the power to remain) during a simulated "Midnight Season"?

- **Grading Matrix:**

    o **Level 1 (The Bottleneck):** The mission dies if they are absent. They hoard authority to feel "needed."

    o **Level 3 (The Steward):** Willing to leave, but has not yet built the infrastructure for the mission to thrive without them.

    o **Level 5 (The Finisher):** Has successfully "killed" their own role. They lead for the **Cloud of Witnesses**, making their own earthly presence secondary to the Mission's longevity.

APPENDIX D

THE 4 Cs INSTITUTIONAL AUDIT & GRADING SYSTEM

A Diagnostic Framework for Sovereign Organizations

Introduction

This audit is designed to measure the "Kingdom Health" of an institution. It moves beyond the carnal metrics of revenue, attendance, and social media reach to examine the **Ontological Infrastructure** of the leadership team.

Instructions

Each section should be scored on a scale of **1 (Saul-Centric)** to **5 (Christ-Centric)**. To reach a "Sovereign Strike" status, an organization must maintain an average score of 4.5 across all four dimensions.

DIMENSION 1: THE CHARACTER ARCHITECTURE (TAMIYM)

Theological Baseline: *"For the eyes of the Lord run to and fro throughout the whole earth, to show Himself strong on behalf of those whose heart is loyal to Him."* (2 Chronicles 16:9)

Metric 1.1: The Transparency Quotient

- **The Audit:** Is there a "Hidden Economy" in the leadership? Are financial decisions, moral failures, or strategic shifts hidden behind a veil of "Executive Privilege"?

- **The Sovereign Standard:** A Level 5 organization has "Glass Walls." While maintaining wisdom and privacy, there is no "Shadow Culture" where secrets are used as currency.

- **Grading Score:** [ ]

Metric 1.2: Image vs. Identity Stewardship

- **The Audit:** How much of the institutional budget and staff time is spent on "Brand Management" and "Public Perception" versus "Internal Formation"?

- **The Sovereign Standard:** In a Level 5 institution, the "Brand" is a byproduct of the "Being." Marketing is secondary to Mission. The organization is comfortable being misunderstood if it means remaining faithful to the Raw Word.

- **Grading Score:** [ ]

DIMENSION 2: THE COMPETENCE SYMMETRY (LION-LAMB)

Theological Baseline: *"He chose David his servant... with upright heart he shepherded them and guided them with his skillful hand."* (Psalm 78:70-72)

Metric 2.1: The Braid Efficiency (Conflict Resolution)

- **The Audit:** When toxicity appears in the team, how long does it take for a "Braid the Cord" intervention to occur? Is

- conflict avoided (The Doormat Lamb) or is it explosive and reactive (The Carnal Lion)?
- **The Sovereign Standard:** Level 5 leaders identify "Money Changers" early. They execute "Surgical Strikes" against bad behavior without destroying the person's dignity.

- **Grading Score:** [ ]

Metric 2.2: The Excellence-to-Anointing Ratio

The Audit: Does the organization "wing it" on anointing to cover up for a lack of rofessional excellence? Are meetings, finances, and communications sloppy?

- **The Sovereign Standard:** Professionalism is treated as a form of worship. The organization is "World Class" in its craft so that the message of Christ is never mocked due to the incompetence of the medium.

- **Grading Score:** [ ]

DIMENSION 3: THE CALLING MULTIPLICATION (TRANSFUSION)

Theological Baseline: *"And the things you have heard me say in the presence of many witnesses entrust to reliable people who will also be qualified to teach others."* (2 Timothy 2:2)

Metric 3.1: Selective Intimacy Implementation

- **The Audit:** Is the Senior Leader's time consumed by the "Many" (The Crowd) or the "Few" (The Successors)? Is there a formal mechanism for DNA Transfusion?

- **The Sovereign Standard:** A Level 5 leader spends 60-80% of their "Spiritual Venture Capital" on their Inner Circle. The organization values "Deep Water" discipleship over "Broad Water" networking.

- **Grading Score:** [ ]

Metric 3.2: The Callous Recruitment Index

- **The Audit:** Does the HR/Recruitment process favor "Polished Pedigrees" (Degrees, Charisma, Status) or "Hidden Callouses" (Grit, Endurance, History of Hiddenness)?

- **The Sovereign Standard:** The organization actively seeks out "Agrammatos" (unlettered) leaders who have proven their faithfulness in the wilderness.

- **Grading Score:** [ ]

DIMENSION 4: THE COMMITMENT LEGACY (TETELESTAI)

Theological Baseline: *"I have glorified You on the earth. I have finished the work which You have given Me to do."* (John 17:4)

Metric 4.1: The Obsolescence Factor

- **The Audit:** If the primary leader were removed today, would the mission expand or contract? Is the vision "FounderDependent" or "DNA-Dependent"?

- **The Sovereign Standard:** A Level 5 organization has a "Cruciform Exit" strategy for every key role. Succession is not an afterthought; it is a daily discipline.

- **Grading Score:** [ ]

Metric 4.2: The Gethsemane Grit Score

- **The Audit:** How does the institution behave during a "Midnight Season" (Financial drought, persecution, or loss of popularity)? Do the leaders flee or do they stay?

- **The Sovereign Standard:** The institution possesses *Hupomonē* (The power to remain). It is not "Mercenary"

- (working for the reward) but "Covenantal" (working for the King).

- **Grading Score:** [ ]

SCORING EVALUATION:

- **08–15: THE SAUL REGIME.** High risk of collapse. Leadership is image-driven and brittle. Immediate repentance and restructuring required.

- **16–25: THE MENTORING TRANSITION.** There is potential, but the "Gap" is still too wide. Competence is high, but Character is lagging.

- **26–35: THE SOVEREIGN STRIKE.** The organization is a lethal weapon in the Kingdom. It is empty of ego and full of authority. It is ready for explosive, multi-generational expansion.

APPENDIX E

The "Institutional Health" Audit

A Diagnostic Framework for Sovereign Organizations

PAGE 1: THE SAUL-REGIME DIAGNOSTIC

Instruction: Rank your organization on a scale of 1 (Saul/Status Quo) to 10 (Sovereign/Kingdom). Provide honest evidence for your score.

1. Identity: Arche vs. Doulos
Do leaders lead from positional power (rights) or bondservant responsibility?

- **Evidence/Observations:** _______________________________
- [SCORE: _____]

2. Information: Image-Spin vs. Radical Integrity
Is truth suppressed to protect the leader's image or shared to protect the mission?
- **Evidence/Observations:** _______________________________
- [SCORE: _____]

3. Succession: Hoarding vs. The Cruciform Exit
Is there an active, joyful plan to make the current leadership obsolete?
- **Evidence/Observations:** _______________________________
- [SCORE: _____]

4. Recruitment: Resume Shine vs. Hidden Callouses
Are you hiring for "Cultural Clones" or those tested by the fire of the wilderness?
- **Evidence/Observations:** _______________________________
- [SCORE: _____]

PAGE 2: THE TOTAL REVERSAL ROADMAP

Use this table to identify where your institution sits in the transition.

Metric	The Saul-Regime (1–3)	The Sovereign Model (8–10)
Identity	**Title-Driven:** Needs to be "The Expert" to feel secure.	**Towel-Driven:** Acts as "The Resource" to empower others.
Information	**Image Management:** Uses spin and "need-to-know" filters.	**Radical Transparency:** Shared data, even when it stings.
Succession	**Legacy Hoarding:** Views talented heirs as threats.	**Cruciform Exit:** Joy in being replaced by trained heirs.
Recruitment	**Surface Polish:** Hiring based on pedigree and "fit."	**Spiritual Grit:** Hiring based on "Hidden Callouses."

PAGE 3: THE TRANSITION WORKSHEET

The "Lethal Strike" requires action. Complete these commitments for your organization.

1. Identify the Spear

In which category did you score the lowest? What specific fear is keeping you in the Saul-Regime in this area?

____

2. The Cruciform Commitment

What is one "right" or "piece of information" your leadership team will release this month to move toward a Doulos posture?

____

3. Calling the Cloud

Who is a "Hidden Calloused" individual in your orbit that you have overlooked? How will you empower them this week?

____

APPENDIX F

THE SOVEREIGN DIALOGUE & FACILITATION TOOLKIT

PART 1: THE SOVEREIGN DIALOGUE (Individual Focus)

Focus: Personal Relinquishment

- **Kenosis:** Identifying the "space" you fill that belongs to others.
- **The Braid:** Moving from reactive anger to prayerful, premeditated discipline.
- **The Agrammatos:** Auditing your heart for "callouses over credentials."
- **The Cruciform Exit:** Preparing your soul to become obsolete for the sake of the mission.

PART 2: THE LEADER'S FACILITATION GUIDE (Organizational Focus)

Focus: Structural Transformation

- **Identity (Arche vs. Doulos):** Moving from positional power to moral authority.
- **Information (Image vs. Integrity):** Killing the "Shadow

Culture" to allow radical honesty.

- **Succession (The Legacy):** Identifying where you are "bottlenecking" the next generation.

- **Recruitment (The Grit):** Choosing the "Third Day" people who can endure the weight of the call.

Facilitating the Saul-Regime Audit

This guide provides the "Why it Matters" and the "Hidden Trap" for each diagnostic category. Use these talking points to deepen the conversation during your next leadership session.

1.   **Identity: Arche vs. Doulos**

- **The Talking Point:** "Are we a team that demands respect because of the boxes on our org chart, or are we a team that earns influence by how well we support those under us?"

- **The Goal:** To move from Positional Authority (I say so because I'm the boss) to Moral Authority (I say so because I am committed to your success).

- **The Question for the Room:** *"If we lost our titles tomorrow, would anyone still follow our lead?"*

2.   **Information: Image vs. Integrity**

- **The Talking Point:** "In a Saul-Regime, 'bad news' is treated as a threat to the leader's ego. In a Sovereign Model, 'bad news' is treated as a diagnostic tool for the mission."

- **The Goal:** To eliminate the "Tax of Deception." When people are afraid to tell the truth, the organization moves slower and makes poorer decisions.

- **The Question for the Room:** *"What is the one thing everyone knows is broken, but no one is allowed to talk about in this meeting?*

3.   **Succession: The Cruciform ExitThe Talking Point:** "A leader's greatest success isn't what they build; it's what continues after they leave. If the organization collapses when you take a vacation, you haven't built a Kingdom; you've built a cage."

- **The Goal:** To replace the "Fear of Irrelevance" with the "Legacy of Empowerment."
- **The Question for the Room:** *"Who are we currently 'bottlenecking' because we are unwilling to hand over the keys to a specific project or decision?"*

4.   **Recruitment: Shine vs. Callouses**

- **The Talking Point:** "Resumes tell us what someone has done; callouses tell us what someone can endure. We are looking for 'The Third Day' people—those who have seen a 'Friday' (failure/death) and stayed long enough for a 'Sunday' (resurrection/growth)."
- **The Goal:** To prioritize Resilience over Aesthetics.
- **The Question for the Room:** *"Are we hiring people who make us look good, or people who have the scars necessary to carry the weight of this mission?"*

PART 3: THE SOVEREIGN COMMITMENT (The Final Action)

1. **The Spear:** Which area of our organization is currently most like the "Saul Regime"?

2. **The Strike:** What is one specific authority I am relinquishing today?

3. **The Transfusion:** Which "Hidden Calloused" leader am I inviting to the table this month?

To conclude the audit, move from diagnosis to action:

1. **Identify the Spear:** Which category scored the

    lowest today? ___________________________________.

2. **The Sovereign Strike:** What is one "right" or "piece of information" our leadership team can release this month to move toward a Doulos posture? ___________________________.

3. **Calling the Cloud:** Who are the "Hidden Calloused" individuals in our orbit we have overlooked? Name one person to empower

    this week: ___________________________________.

APPENDIX G

The Leader's Quick-Reference Rubric

The Final Hierarchy for Your Manuscript

OPERATIONAL FRAMEWORK FOR CHRIST-CENTERED LEADERSHIP

Title: THE LETHAL STRIKE: A Blueprint for Sovereign Leadership and the Four Cs

Author: Laeticia Amaka Anene

Core Objective: To provide a tactical and theological roadmap for dismantling the "Saul Regime" and establishing the "Sovereign Strike" in organizational leadership.

PART I: FOUNDATIONS & THE ONTOLOGICAL SHIFT

- **Chapter 1: The Vacuum of Power** *Thesis:* Leadership begins with *Kenosis* (self-emptying). Success is found in creating a functional vacuum where the ego once sat, allowing God's authority to fill the void.

- **Chapter 2: Holy Friction (The Lamb with a Whip)** *Thesis:* Service is not passivity. Competence requires the "Symmetry of the Scars"—the ability to switch between washing feet and flipping tables in the same hour.

PART V: THE FOURTH C – COMMITMENT & LEGACY

- **Chapter 9: Testing and the Gethsemane Grit** *Thesis:* Commitment is revealed in the garden of suffering, not on the mountaintop. Endurance is the "Lethal Strike" against the enemy.

- **Chapter 10: The Cruciform Exit** *Thesis:* The ultimate goal of leadership is to become obsolete. Success is measured by how the mission functions when you are gone (*Tetelestai*).

THE INSTITUTIONAL TOOLKIT

1. **Appendix A:** The 12-Week Syllabus (For seminaries and leadership teams).

2. **Appendix B:** The Formation Rubric (A diagnostic tool for Lion vs. Lamb Symmetry).

3. **The Sovereign Strike Cheat Sheet:** A 4 Cs Field Guide for Rapid Tactical Recall.

Appendix F

The Glossary of the Strike

- **Agrammatos (Gr. ἀγράμματος):** Literally "unlettered." The status of the Apostles in Acts 4:13. It is not a lack of intelligence, but a lack of *Regime-indoctrination.*

- **Arche (Gr. ἀρχή):** Positional authority or "beginning." In the Saul-Regime, leaders cling to *Arche* as a right. In the Sovereign Strike, *Arche* is surrendered for the mission.

- **The Cloud:** The space of divine presence that is vacated when an institution becomes obsessed with its own image. To "Call the Cloud" is to invite the Holy Spirit back into the vacuum of human surrender.

- **Doulos (Gr. δοῦλος):** A bondservant. The ultimate posture of the Sovereign Leader. Unlike a hireling, the *Doulos* has no rights, only a Master.

- **Hidden Callouses:** The spiritual markers of those who have survived the "Wilderness" or the "Nothing." These are the primary recruits for the Strike.

- **Kenosis (Gr. κένωσις):** The act of self-emptying. Based on Philippians 2, it is the voluntary renunciation of power and status to achieve a higher Kingdom purpose.

- **Lethal Strike:** A surgical, decisive action that dismantles institutional pride and restores the Sovereign flow of the Gospel.

- **The Nothing:** The uncomfortable gap between "The End of the Regime" and "The Birth of the New." It is the space where the Strike is most effective.

- **Saul-Regime:** Any leadership structure—ecclesiastical or corporate—that prioritizes its own survival, image management, and power hoarding over the Divine Will.

- **Tamiym (Heb. תָּמִים):** Blameless or "complete." Not a state of sinless perfection, but a state of absolute integrity where the internal heart matches the external action.

1.   The Seminary Discussion Guide (The "Must-Read" Factor)

SOVEREIGN DIALOGUE: Deep-Dive Questions for Leadership Cohorts

1. **On Kenosis:** In your current leadership role, what "space" are you filling that should be left as a vacuum for others (or for God) to occupy?

2. **On the Braid:** When was the last time you "braided a cord" (premeditated discipline) versus reacting out of carnal frustration?

3. **On the Agrammatos:** Look at your recruitment pipeline. Are you unintentionally filtering out the "Calloused Available" in favor of the "Polished Elite"?

4. **On the Exit:** If you were removed from your organization tomorrow, what specific systems would fail? Does that reveal your strength as a leader, or your failure as a Christ-model?

2.　High-Impact Press Release Headline

(The "Lethal Strike" Media Hook)

FOR IMMEDIATE RELEASE

The Saul Regime is Dead: New Leadership Blueprint

Challenges the Cult of the 'Full' Executive"

rtesia, CA — With the launch of *THE LETHAL STRIKE*, author Laeticia Amaka Anene issues a surgical strike against the modern obsession with personal branding and executive ego. Moving beyond corporate clichés, Anene introduces the "Sovereign Nothing"—a leader defined not by the space they take up, but by the vacuum they create for Divine authority to fill. At a time when leadership trust is at an all-time low, this "field manual" offers the radical return to the Lion-Lamb symmetry that the 21st-century church and marketplace have been waiting for.

3.   The "Institutional Health" Audit (The Boardroom Tool)

THE SAUL-REGIME DIAGNOSTIC

Rank your organization on a scale of 1 (Saul/Status Quo) to 10 (Sovereign/Kingdom):

1. **Identity:** Do our leaders lead from their *Arche* (Title) or their *Doulos* (Bondservant) status? [ ]

2. **Information:** Is truth suppressed to protect the leader's image? [ ]

3. **Succession:** Is there a "Cruciform Exit" (making oneself obsolete) actively being planned? [ ]

4. **Recruitment:** Are we hiring for "Resume Shine" or "Hidden Callouses"? [ ]

SCORING:

- **0-10:** *Saul's Palace.* Urgent intervention required.

- **11-30:** *Wilderness Shift.* The process of emptying has begun.

- **31-40:** *Sovereign Strike Readiness.* You are moving in the authority of the Cloud.

THE LEADERSHIP WORKSHOP

FROM SAUL TO SOVEREIGN

PART 1: THE SOVEREIGN DIALOGUE (The Leader's Soul)

Focus: Personal Relinquishment

- **Kenosis:** Identifying the "space" you fill that belongs to others.
- **The Braid:** Moving from reactive anger to prayerful, premeditated discipline.
- **The Agrammatos:** Auditing your heart for "callouses over credentials."
- **The Cruciform Exit:** Preparing your soul to become obsolete for the sake of the mission.

PART 2:   THE FACILITATION GUIDE (The Organization's Health)

Focus: Structural Transformation

- **Identity (Arche vs. Doulos):** Moving from positional power to moral authority.

- **Information (Image vs. Integrity):** Killing the "Shadow Culture" to allow radical honesty.

- **Succession (The Legacy):** Identifying where you are "bottlenecking" the next generation.

- **Recruitment (The Grit):** Choosing the "Third Day" people who can endure the weight of the call.

PART 3: THE SOVEREIGN COMMITMENT (The Final Action)

1. **The Spear:** Which area of our organization is currently most like the "Saul Regime"?
2. **The Strike:** What is one specific authority I am relinquishing today?
3. **The Transfusion:** Which "Hidden Calloused" leader am I inviting to the table this month?

Final Checklist for Tomorrow:

- **Flyer:** Hand out only after a conversation starts.
- **Bio:** Use the **"Frontline Strategist"** version (Option 2).
- **The Audit:** Mention the **"Saul-Regime Audit"** to executives—it's a high-value "hook" for future partnerships.

THE LEADER'S GUIDE

Facilitating the Saul-Regime Audit

This guide provides the "Why it Matters" and the "Hidden Trap" for each of the four diagnostic questions. Use these talking points to deepen the conversation during your next leadership session.

1. Identity: Arche vs. Doulos

- **The Talking Point:** "Are we a team that demands respect because of the boxes on our org chart, or are we a team that earns influence by how well we support those under us?"

- **The Goal:** To move from **Positional Authority** (I say so because I'm the boss) to **Moral Authority** (I say so because I am committed to your success).

- **The Question for the Room:** *"If we lost our titles tomorrow, would anyone still follow our lead?"*

2. Information: Image vs. Integrity

- **The Talking Point:** "In a Saul-Regime, 'bad news' is treated as a threat to the leader's ego. In a Sovereign Model, 'bad news' is treated as a diagnostic tool for the mission."

- **The Goal:** To eliminate the "Tax of Deception." When people are afraid to tell the truth, the organization moves slower and makes poorer decisions.

- **The Question for the Room:** *"What is the one thing everyone knows is broken, but no one is allowed to talk about in this meeting?"*

3. Succession: The Cruciform Exit

- **The Talking Point:** "A leader's greatest success isn't what they build; it's what continues after they leave. If the organization collapses when you take a vacation, you haven't built a Kingdom; you've built a cage."

- **The Goal:** To replace the "Fear of Irrelevance" with the "Legacy of Empowerment."

- **The Question for the Room:** *"Who are we currently 'bottlenecking' because we are unwilling to hand over the keys to a specific project or decision?"*

4. Recruitment: Shine vs. Callouses

- **The Talking Point:** "Resumes tell us what someone has done; callouses tell us what someone can endure. We are looking for 'The Third Day' people—those who have seen a 'Friday' (failure/death) and stayed long enough for a 'Sunday' (resurrection/growth)."

- **The Goal:** To prioritize **Resilience** over **Aesthetics**.

- **The Question for the Room:** *"Are we hiring people who make us look good, or people who have the scars necessary to carry the weight of this mission?"*

Closing the Audit

To wrap up the session, ask each leader to commit to one **"Sovereign Strike"**: A single, immediate action that kills a "Saul" habit within their department.

THE SAUL-REGIME DIAGNOSTIC

Rank your organization on a scale of **1 (Saul/Status Quo)** to **10 (Sovereign/Kingdom)**:

1. **Identity:** Do our leaders lead from their *Arche* (Title/Rights) or their *Doulos* (Bondservant/Responsibilities) status? [ ]

2. **Information:** Is truth suppressed to protect the leader's image, or is transparency prioritized to protect the mission's integrity? [ ]

3. **Succession:** Is there a "Cruciform Exit" (the intentional process of making oneself obsolete) actively being planned and executed? [ ]

4. **Recruitment:** Are we hiring for "Resume Shine" (Pedigree/Optics) or "Hidden Callouses" (Character/Proven Suffering)? [ ]

SCORING & INTERPRETATION

- **0–10: Saul's Palace** | *Urgent intervention required.* The institution is currently designed to bypass the Cross in favor of comfort and control. Leadership is likely personalitydriven and fragile.

- **11–30: Wilderness Shift** | *The process of emptying has begun.* You are in the "in-between" stage. You have recognized the bankruptcy of the status quo but have not yet fully integrated the new metrics of Kingdom authority.

- **31–40: Sovereign Strike Readiness** | *Moving in the authority of the **Cloud of Witnesses.*** You have moved from "Protecting the Throne" to "Extending the Kingdom."

The organization is healthy, decentralized, and built for a legacy that outlives its current leaders.

THE TOTAL REVERSAL (The Roadmap to Health)

To move your score toward **Sovereign Strike Readiness**, apply these structural reversals:

Metric	The Saul-Regime (1–3)	The Sovereign Model (8–10)
Identity	**Title-Driven:** Highcontrol; needs to be "The Expert" to feel secure.	**Tow-Driven:** High-trust; acts as "The Resource" to empower others.
Information	**Image Management:** Use of spin-doctoring, silos, and "need-toknow" filters.	**Radical Transparency:** Shared data and honest assessments, even when they sting.
Succession	**Legacy Hoarding:** Fear of replacement; view of talented subordinates as threats.	**The Cruciform Exit:** Joy in being replaced; actively training heirs to go further than you.
Recruitment	**Surface Polish:** Hiring based on cultural "fit," clones, and impressive resumes.	**Spiritual Grit:** Hiring based on "Hidden Callouses"—those tested by failure and fire.

TRANSITION WORKSHEET

From Saul to Sovereign

1. Identify the Spear: In which of the four categories did we score the lowest? What specific "fear" is keeping us in the Saul-Regime in this area?

Response: ____

2. The Cruciform Commitment: What is one "right" or "piece of information" our leadership team can release this month to move toward a *Doulos* (servant) posture?

Response: ____

3. Calling the Cloud: Who are the "Hidden Calloused" individuals already in our orbit that we have overlooked because they lack "Resume Shine"?

Response: ____

THE SEMINARY DISCUSSION GUIDE

SOVEREIGN DIALOGUE

SYLLABUS & READING LIST

1. On Kenosis (Self-Emptying)

- **The Concept:** The voluntary relinquishing of divine/personal prerogatives to become a servant. It is not the loss of power, but the refusal to use power for self-preservation.

- **The Text: Philippians 2:5–8.** *"Have this mind among yourselves... who, though he was in the form of God, did not count equality with God a thing to be grasped, but emptied himself..."*

- **Key Question:** Are you using your leadership "rights" to protect your position, or are you "emptying" your schedule and authority to create room for others to lead?

2. On the Braid (Premeditated Discipline)

- **The Concept:** The distinction between "Carnal Reactivity" and "Sovereign Zeal." Jesus did not lose His temper in the Temple; He performed a controlled, intentional act of justice that required the time it took to physically braid a whip.

- **The Text: John 2:13–17.** *"...and making a whip of cords, he* *drove them all out of the temple..."*

- **Key Question:** How much of your current "discipline" of staff or systems is a sudden reaction to frustration versus a prayerfully "braided" response designed for long-term correction?

3. On the Agrammatos (The Ordinary Catalyst)

- **The Concept:** God's consistent pattern of bypassing the credentialed elite to find the "calloused available." *Agrammatos* does not mean "ignorant," but specifically refers to those outside the formal academic/power structures of the day.

- **The Text: Acts 4:13.** *"Now when they saw the boldness of Peter and John, and perceived that they were uneducated (agrammatos) and common men, they were astonished. And they recognized that they had been with Jesus."*

- **Key Question:** Is your "Succession Pipeline" biased toward those with the best degrees, or those with the most "boldness" and evidence of "having been with Jesus"?

The Sovereign Dialogue

A Seminary & Leadership Guide

Designed for Leadership Cohorts, Elders, and Executive Teams.

I. Key Terminology

- **Kenosis:** The "self-emptying" of Christ (Phil 2:7). The refusal to use power for self-preservation.

- **Agrammatos:** The Greek term for "unlettered" or

- "uneducated" (Acts 4:13). It refers to those outside formal power structures who carry spiritual authority.

- **The Braid:** A reference to Jesus braiding the whip (John 2:15)—an act of premeditated, controlled justice rather than a reactive loss of temper.

II. The Deep-Dive Modules

1. On Kenosis (The Self-Emptying)

- **The Concept:** The voluntary relinquishing of personal prerogatives to become a servant.
- **The Text:** Philippians 2:5–8.

- **The Diagnostic:** In your current leadership role, what "space" are you filling that should be left as a vacuum for others—or for God—to occupy?

- **The Goal:** To identify where your "competence" has become a "crutch" that prevents others from growing.

2. On the Braid (Premeditated Discipline)

- **The Concept:** The distinction between "Carnal Reactivity" and "Sovereign Zeal."

- **The Text:** John 2:13–17.

- **The Diagnostic:** When was the last time you "braided a cord"—utilizing prayerful discipline—versus reacting out of carnal frustration or immediate "firefighting"?

- **The Goal:** To distinguish between righteous zeal (which is prepared) and unbridled anger (which is reactive).

3. On the Agrammatos (The Ordinary Catalyst)

- **The Concept:** God's pattern of bypassing the credentialed elite to find the "calloused available."

- **The Text:** Acts 4:13.

- **The Diagnostic:** Are you unintentionally filtering out the *Agrammatos* in your recruitment pipeline in favor of the "Polished Elite"?

- **The Goal:** To prioritize evidence of "having been with Jesus" over formal academic credentials alone.

4. On the Exit (The Cruciform Legacy)

- **The Concept:** The "Success of the Successor." A leader's legacy is measured by the health of the organization after their departure.

- **The Text:** <u>John 16:7</u>.

- **The Diagnostic:** If you were removed tomorrow, what specific systems would fail? Does that failure reveal your strength, or your failure to make yourself obsolete?

- **The Goal:** To measure the health of your "Cruciform Exit."

III. The Synthesis: Sovereign Commitment

Move from Dialogue to Doing by answering the following:

- **The Relinquishment:** Based on *Kenosis*, what specific power or decision will I "empty" myself of this week?

- **The Observation:** Based on *Agrammatos*, who in my periphery will I invite to the table this month?

- **The Prayer of the Braid:** *"Lord, give me the patience to braid the cord before I enter the temple. Let my discipline be intentional, not impulsive."*

Cohort Closing Prayer "Lord, deliver us from the palace of Saul. Teach us the patience of the Braid, the humility of Kenosis, the eye for the Agrammatos, and the courage of the Cruciform Exit. May we be leaders who move in the authority of the Cloud of Witnesses, rather than the insecurity of our own names. Amen."

CASE STUDY I

THE ANATOMY OF A KENOTIC TAKEOVER

Focus: Part I (Identity) & Part II (Character)

Subject: Elias Thorne, Marketplace Executive (Fortune 500 Context) The Context

E lias Thorne was recruited as the CEO of a failing global logistics firm. The culture was a "Shadow of Saul" environment: the previous leadership had built a cult of personality, hoarding information and leading through intimidation. The "Gap" between the company's public marketing (innovation and care) and its internal reality (fear and stagnation) was a chasm.

The Sovereign Strike:

Instead of the typical "First 100 Days" strategy of asserting dominance, Elias performed a **Vacuum of Power** maneuver. He spent the first 30 days in silence. He moved his office from the top floor to a cubicle near the loading docks. He refused the "Executive Perk" package, opting to eat in the communal cafeteria.

The Holy Friction:

Elias identified the "Money Changers" in the VP layer—three executives who were hitting their financial targets but destroying the human capital of their departments. One VP, a brilliant but tyrannical strategist, mocked Elias's "servant" approach. Elias spent two weeks **"Braiding the Cord."** He didn't fire the VP in a fit of rage. He gathered the data of the turnover rates and the exit interviews. In a calm, 15-minute meeting, Elias presented the "Symmetry of Authority." He told the VP, *"Your results are excellent, but your fruit is rotten. You have turned this department into a paywall for our people's potential. Today, the tables are being flipped."* Elias fired the high-performer publicly to signal a culture shift toward **Tamiym** (Wholeness).

The Result:

By becoming a "Sovereign Nothing," Elias removed the ceiling of fear. Within 18 months, the company saw a 40% increase in employee-led innovation. Elias's legacy wasn't that he "saved" the company, but that he created a vacuum where others were finally free to lead.

CASE STUDY II

THE RECRUITMENT OF THE "NOBODIES"

Focus: Part III (Competence) & Part IV (Calling)

Subject: Marcus Vane, Church Planter(Urban Frontier Context)

The Context

Marcus was planting a church in a "volatile intersection" of a major city. Every church planting manual told him to recruit "The Best and the Brightest"—musicians with professional reels, administrators with MBAs, and social media influencers to "build the buzz."

The Sovereign Strike:
Marcus rejected the "Credentialed Elite." He remembered the **Recruitment Paradox**. He spent his time at the local laundromat and the public basketball courts. He wasn't looking for "Full" leaders; he was looking for **Callouses.**

The Transfusion

He found "Sarah," a single mother who had worked two jobs for a decade without a single complaint, and "Julian," a former gang member who had spent five years in "hidden" ministry in the local prison. Neither had a seminary degree. Both were *Agrammatos* (unlettered) in the eyes of the institutional church.

Marcus practiced **Selective Intimacy.** He spent 15 hours a week with Sarah and Julian, not teaching them "Church Growth Tactics," but transfusing the **Identity of Christ.** He allowed them to see his own Gethsemane moments when the funding was low.

The Result

When a major crisis hit the neighborhood (a localized riot), the "Professional" churches in the area closed their doors to protect their assets. Sarah and Julian, however, stayed on the streets. They had the **Grit of the Docks.** Because Marcus had invested in "Nobodies," the church became a "Sovereign Something" in the heart of the city. They didn't have a brand; they had a **Burden.**

CASE STUDY III

THE CRUCIFORM EXIT OF THE REFORMER

Focus: Part V (Commitment & Legacy)

Subject: Historical Case Study: Count Nikolaus von Zinzendorf (The Moravian Move)

The Context

In the 18th century, Zinzendorf was a nobleman with vast wealth and social status. He founded the "Herrnhut" community—a refuge for persecuted Christians. As the leader, he could have easily built a "Zinzendorf Brand."

The Sovereign Strike

Zinzendorf understood the **Cruciform Exit** better than almost any leader in history. He realized that for the mission to go global, he had to become obsolete. He didn't want to be the "CEO of the Moravians." He wanted to be a **Bondservant.**

The "It Is Finished" Strategy

He instituted a 24/7 prayer chain that lasted for 100 years. Crucially, he did not lead the prayer meetings. He trained "laypeople"—cobblers, smiths, and farmers—to carry the spiritual weight. When it came time to send missionaries to the West Indies, Zinzendorf didn't go. He sent "Nobodies" who were willing to sell themselves into slavery just to reach the enslaved.

The Result

Zinzendorf died in 1760. Most movements die within 10 years of the founder's death. But because Zinzendorf had mastered **Designing Obsolescence**, the Moravian movement exploded after he was gone. His **Commitment** wasn't to his position; it was to the DNA transfusion. John Wesley, the founder of Methodism, was eventually converted through the legacy of the people Zinzendorf had "emptied" himself for. Zinzendorf died a "Sovereign Nothing," yet his "Lethal Strike" changed the course of church history.

THE 12-MONTH EXECUTIVE DEVOTIONAL

THE SOVEREIGN STRIKE

JANUARY: The Month of the Vacuum

- **The Focus:** *Kenosis* (Self-Emptying).

- **The Raw Word:** *"He must increase, but I must decrease."* (John 3:30)

- **The Reflection:** Most leaders start the year with "More"—more goals, more vision, more expansion. But the Christ leader starts with "Less." This month, identify the areas of your leadership where your "Self" has become a ceiling for the Spirit. You cannot be filled with the new wine of the coming year if you are still full of last year's reputation.

- **The Strike:** Cancel one "ego-project" this month. Choose to be "Nothing" in one specific meeting so that God can be "Everything."

FEBRUARY: The Month of the Tamiym Heart

- **The Focus:** Integrity as Architecture.

- **The Raw Word:** *"The integrity of the upright guides them."* (Proverbs 11:3).

- **The Reflection:** Integrity is not just "not lying." It is the structural wholeness of your soul. This month, audit the "Gap" between your public rhetoric and your private reality. If you are preaching about prayer but haven't spoken to the Father in a week, you have a structural flaw.

- **The Strike:** Spend one full day in silence. No phone. No Bible. Just you and the Creator. Let the "noise" of your insecurities rise so they can be dealt with at the root.

MARCH: The Month of the Braid

- **The Focus:** Premeditated Discipline.

- **The Raw Word:** *"And making a whip of cords..."* (John 2:15)

- **The Reflection:** Conflict is a stewardship. Many leaders avoid the "Whip" because they want to be liked. But the Christ-leader knows that unaddressed toxicity is a sin against the sheep. This month, identify the "Money Changers" in your organization—the processes or people desecrating the mission.

- **The Strike:** Braid your cord. Prepare for one difficult, surgical conversation. Execute it with 100% mission-clarity and 0% emotional heat.

APRIL: The Month of the Towel

- **The Focus:** The Symmetry of Authority.

- **The Raw Word:** *"He began to wash his disciples' feet."* (John 13:5).

- **The Reflection:** Your right to flip a table is earned by your willingness to wash a foot. Power without sacrifice is tyranny. This month, look for the "lowest" task in your organization. Do it without announcing it on social media.

- **The Strike:** Perform a service for a subordinate that is "beneath" your pay grade. Do it in secret.

MAY: The Month of the Net-Washing

- **The Focus:** Grit over Gift.

- **The Raw Word:** *"But the disciples were washing their nets."* (Luke 5:2).

- **The Reflection:** We celebrate the "Catch," but God celebrates the "Wash." Anyone can lead when the nets are full. A Sovereign Leader is formed in the mundane, hidden work of preparation. This month, honor the "Net-Washers" in your life—those who do the dirty work while you are on the stage.

- **The Strike:** Find a "hidden" faithful worker in your team and give them a public seat of honor this month.

JUNE: The Month of Selective Intimacy

- **The Focus:** The Strategy of Transfusion.

- **The Raw Word:** *"He chose twelve..."* (Mark 3:14)

- **The Reflection:** You cannot lead everyone. If you try to reach the masses, you will fail the few. This month, evaluate your "Inner Circle." Are you spending your "Venture Capital of the Soul" on those who will carry the DNA of the mission forward?

- **The Strike:** Cancel a broad "networking" event and spend four hours in deep-water conversation with one emerging leader.

JULY: The Month of the Desert

- **The Focus:** Leading through the Wilderness.

- **The Raw Word:** *"Jesus was led by the Spirit into the wilderness."* (Matthew 4:1)

- **The Reflection:** The wilderness is not a detour; it is the training ground for authority. If you are in a dry season where resources are thin, do not panic. God is stripping away your reliance on "Fullness" so you can master the "Nothing."
- **The Strike:** When you feel the urge to "hustle" out of a dry season, choose instead to "wait." Rely on the Word, not the Work.

AUGUST: The Month of Callouses

- **The Focus:** Hiring for Grit.

- **The Raw Word:** *"But they were unlettered and common men."* (Acts 4:13)

- **The Reflection:** Stop being impressed by credentials. Start being impressed by scars. This month, look at your recruitment strategy. Are you hiring "polished" mercenaries or "calloused" bondservants?

- **The Strike:** Interview someone for a role without looking at their degree. Ask them only about their failures and how they survived them.

SEPTEMBER: The Month of the Paywall

- **The Focus:** Removing Obstructions.

- **The Raw Word:** *"Remove the stones."* (John 11:39)

- **The Reflection:** Institutional leaders often become stonecollectors. We create policies and traditions that act as paywalls to the Presence. This month, identify one "stone" in your

- organization that is making it harder for "Nobodies" to reach the Master.

- **The Strike:** Kill one outdated program or policy that serves the "system" but hinders the "sheep."

OCTOBER: The Month of the Image-Death

- **The Focus:** Reputation Fasting.
- **The Raw Word:** *"He made himself of no reputation."* (Philippians 2:7)

- **The Reflection:** Your "Brand" is a cage. When you lead to protect your image, you are a prisoner of the crowd's opinion. This month, embrace being misunderstood. Do the right thing even if it "looks" wrong to the critics.

- **The Strike:** If you are unfairly criticized this month, **do not defend yourself.** Let your identity in Christ be your only shield.

NOVEMBER: The Month of Tetelestai

- **The Focus:** Designing Obsolescence.

- **The Raw Word:** *"It is finished."* (John 19:30).

- **The Reflection:** Success is measured by your absence. A leader who cannot leave is a leader who has failed the 4th C (Commitment). This month, begin the work of "Finishing." What keys are you still holding that belong in the hands of others?

- **The Strike:** Identify your "Successor" (even if they don't know it yet) and hand them a significant piece of your authority this month.

DECEMBER: The Month of the Sovereign Strike

- **The Focus:** The Cloud of Witnesses.

- **The Raw Word:** *"Well done, good and faithful servant."* (Matthew 25:21)

- **The Reflection:** We do not lead for the applause of the present; we lead for the evaluation of the Eternal. This month, integrate the 4 Cs. Character, Competence, Calling, and Commitment. You are a "Sovereign Nothing" carrying a "Lethal Strike."

- **The Strike:** Review the year. Where did you lead like Saul? Repent. Where did you THE LETHAL STRIKE? Rejoice. Prepare for a new level of "Nothingness" in the year to come.

The Seminary Discussion Guide
(The "Must Read" Factor)

SOVEREIGN DIALOGUE

Deep-Dive Questions for Leadership Cohorts

On Kenosis:

In your current leadership role, what "space" are you filling that should be left as a vacuum for others (or for God) to occupy?

> **The Goal:** To identify where your "competence" has become a "crutch" that prevents others from growing.

On the Braid:

When was the last time you "braided a cord" (premeditated discipline) versus reacting out of carnal frustration?

> **The Goal: To distinguish between *righteous zeal* (which is prepared) and *unbridled anger* (which is reactive).**

On the Agrammatos

(The Untrained/Ordinary) Look at your recruitment pipeline. Are you unintentionally filtering out the

Agrammatos (the "unlearned" but calloused and available) in favor of the "Polished Elite"?

> **The Goal: To remember that the Apostles were "uneducated and ordinary men" (Acts 4:13) who had been with Jesus.**

On the Exit (The Cruciform Legacy)

If you were removed from your organization tomorrow, what specific systems would fail? Does that failure reveal your strength as an indispensable leader, or your failure as a Christ-model who should be making themselves obsolete?

> **The Goal: To measure the health of your "Cruciform Exit."**

THE SYNTHESIS

FROM DIALOGUE TO DOING

To complete this cohort session, move from the "Discussion" to the **"Sovereign Commitment."** Ask each participant to answer the following:

- **The Relinquishment:** Based on the *Kenosis* question, what specific task or decision-making power will I "empty" myself of this week?

- **The Observation:** Based on the *Agrammatos* question, who in my "periphery" (the calloused but overlooked) will I invite to the table this month?

- **The Prayer of the Braid:** "Lord, give me the patience to braid the cord before I enter the temple. Let my discipline be intentional, not impulsive."

KEY TERMINOLOGY CHECK

- **Kenosis:** The "self-emptying" of Christ (Phil 2:7).

- **Agrammatos:** The Greek term for "unlettered" or "uneducated" used to describe Peter and John in Acts 4.

- **The Braid:** A reference to Jesus braiding the whip of cords (John 2:15)—an act of premeditated, controlled justice rather than a loss of temper.

CASE STUDY I

THE ANATOMY OF A KENOTIC TAKEOVER

Subject: Elias Thorne, Logistics CEO

Theme: Part I & II (Identity & Character)

The Crisis of the Pedestal

Elias Thorne was headhunted to save *Logos Global*, a $4B logistics firm that was hemorrhaging talent. The previous CEO, a "Saul" figure named Marcus Vance, had led by "Fullness." Vance's office was a fortress of mahogany and glass, inaccessible to the "Nobodies" on the warehouse floor. He led through "Image Management," spending millions on branding while the internal infrastructure was rotting.

When Elias arrived, the board expected a "Lion." They expected a man who would walk in, fire 20% of the staff, and re-assert "The Arche" (The Right to Rule). Instead, Elias performed the **Kenosis Protocol**.

The 30-Day Silence

Elias's first "Lethal Strike" was a subtractive one. He moved his desk. He didn't move it to a larger suite; he moved it to a 10x10 cubicle in the middle of the dispatch floor. For the first 30 days, he

issued zero memos. He made zero speeches. He simply sat in the "Vacuum" and listened to the "Net-Washers."

He was practicing the **"Sovereign Nothing."** By refusing to project an image, he forced the toxic elements of the culture to reveal themselves. You see, when a leader is "Empty," the people around them eventually fill that space with their own true nature. The "Money Changers" in the VP layer began to complain about his "lack of presence." They were used to a King they could mirror; they didn't know how to handle a Servant they couldn't manipulate.

The Braid and the VP of Operations

The turning point came with the VP of Operations, Sarah G. Sarah was a "High-Performer." She hit her numbers every quarter, but she did it through a "Culture of Fear." She was the gatekeeper. She had created a "Paywall to the CEO," ensuring that no warehouse worker could ever speak to the top floor without her permission.

Elias spent a week **"Braiding his Cord."** He sat in the cafeteria with the drivers. He documented the "Scars" Sarah had left on the team. He didn't react with carnal anger. He waited until the Monday morning executive briefing.

In front of the entire board, Elias didn't shout. He spoke with the **Symmetry of Authority.** He looked at Sarah and said, *"Your competence with numbers is undeniable. But your competence with people is a desecration of this mission. You have turned the Court of the Gentiles—our dispatch floor—into a place of fear. You are the Paywall. And today, the table is being flipped."* He fired her on the spot. Not because she missed a KPI, but because her **Character** was a structural flaw in the **Institution.**

The Result: The Vacuum Filled

With the "Money Changer" removed, the vacuum Elias had created was suddenly filled by the Spirit of the Mission. Innovation surged. Drivers started suggesting routes that saved the company millions. Because Elias was a "Sovereign Nothing," the "Nobodies" finally became the "Somebodies" who saved the firm.

CASE STUDY II

RECRUITING THE NOBODIES

Subject: Marcus Vane, Church Planter

Theme: Part III & IV (Competence & Calling)

The Failure of the "Dream Team"

Marcus Vane had originally tried to plant *The Summit Church* using the "Credentialed" model. He hired a Worship Leader with a record deal, an Executive Pastor with an MBA, and a social media Director with 100k followers. It was a "Dream Team" of **Fullness.** Within 12 months, the plant imploded. Why? Because the team was full of "Gifts" but had no "Grit." When the "Wilderness" of city-center ministry hit, the mercenaries fled for easier assignments.

The Callous Check at the Basketball Court

Marcus's second attempt was a **Sovereign Strike.** He stopped looking at resumes and started looking at **scars.** He spent six months playing pick-up basketball at a local park. He was looking for **"Net Washers."**

He found "Big Mike." Mike was a middle-aged man who volunteered to clean the park bathrooms every Saturday, simply because "it needed doing." No one thanked him. No one paid him.

No one even knew his name.

Marcus approached him. He didn't ask about his theology; he asked about his **Hupomonē.** *"Why do you stay when everyone else leaves the mess?"* Mike replied, *"I've been through the fire, Pastor. I know how to stay under the weight."*

The Selective Intimacy Protocol

Marcus recruited Mike and two others: a nurse who worked the graveyard shift and a schoolteacher who had spent 20 years in a failing district. These were his **Agrammatos** (unlettered) leaders.

Marcus ignored the "Masses" to focus on these three. He practiced **Selective Intimacy.** He ate with them. He wept with them. He transfused his DNA into them. He wasn't building a "Church Service"; he was building a **Strike Team.**

The Crisis and the Legacy

When a local economic collapse hit the neighborhood, the "Professional" churches nearby struggled to keep their staff. But *The Summit* thrived. Why? Because Marcus's team was **Calloused.** They were used to catching nothing all night and still washing the nets. They didn't lead for the "Crowd of the Present"; they led for the **Cloud of Witnesses.** Because Marcus had the "Sovereign Spine" to choose "Nobodies," he built a "Something" that the gates of hell could not prevail against.

CASE STUDY III

THE CRUCIFORM EXIT OF THE REFORMER

Subject: Count Nikolaus von Zinzendorf & The Moravian Movement

Theme: Part V (Commitment & Legacy)

The Nobleman's Kenosis

In the early 1700s, Nikolaus von Zinzendorf was a man of extreme "Fullness." He was a German Count, a legal scholar, and a member of the royal court of Dresden. By the world's standards, his "Image" was impenetrable. He possessed the *Arche* (the right to rule) by birthright. However, Zinzendorf underwent a **Kenotic Shift**. While viewing a painting of the thorn-crowned Christ (the *Ecce Homo*), he was struck by the "Lethal Strike" of the Savior's sacrifice.

He realized that his title was a "Paywall" to his true calling. He did not merely "step down"; he performed a **Sovereign Vacuum**. He opened his estate, *Herrnhut* ("The Lord's Watch"), to a group of ragged, persecuted refugees. To the elite of Europe, this was a "Reputation Suicide." A Count does not live with "Nobodies." But Zinzendorf had already started leading for the **Cloud of Witnesses.**

The Braid of Herrnhut

The community at Herrnhut was not an immediate utopia. It was a "Temple" filled with "Money Changers" of a different sort: religious pride, sectarian division, and bitter theological arguments. The "Friction" was at an all-time high.

Zinzendorf did not react with "Carnal Anger." He did not use his title to force compliance. Instead, he spent the summer of 1727 **Braiding the Cord.** He went from house to house, washing feet, listening to the "Scars" of the refugees, and drafting a "Brotherly Agreement." This was **Executive Deliberation** at its finest. He didn't attack the people; he attacked the *system* of division.

On August 13, 1727, the "Symmetry of Authority" was achieved. During a communion service, the "Nothingness" of the leader met the "Fullness" of the Spirit. The division broke. Zinzendorf's "Braid" had worked—not because he was a Count, but because he had become a **Bondservant.**

The 100-Year Strike (Succession Mindset)

The greatest mark of Zinzendorf's competence was his **Obsolescence Strategy.** He knew that if the Moravian movement depended on his "Presence," it would die with his pulse.

1. **The Prayer-Transfusion:** He instituted a 24/7 prayer chain. Crucially, he did not lead it. He transfused the "Identity of the Watchman" into the common laborers—the cobblers, the milkmaids, and the smiths. He was practicing **Selective Intimacy** with "Nobodies" who would eventually carry the Gospel to the ends of the earth.

2. **The Slave-Master Move:** When the call came to reach the enslaved people in the West Indies, Zinzendorf did not send "Credentialed Clergy." He sent two common men, Dober and Nitschmann. When they were told they could not reach the

3. slaves unless they became slaves themselves, they famously cried, *"May the Lamb that was slain receive the reward of His suffering!"* This was the **DNA of the Leader** manifesting in the followers.

The Cruciform Exit

Zinzendorf died in 1760. In the decades following his death, the Moravian movement did not contract; it exploded. Because he had mastered the **Cruciform Exit**, the mission was no longer

"Founder Centric." He had designed an organization that functioned better in his absence than in his presence.

He died with "no reputation" among the royals of his day, but he was a "Sovereign" in the eyes of the Cloud. His legacy was not his estate at Herrnhut; it was the fact that a century later, John Wesley—the man who would shake England—was converted through the "Transfused Life" of the Moravians Zinzendorf had trained.

The Lesson for the Modern Leader:

Your "Lethal Strike" is not found in how many people follow you today. It is found in how many people *THE LETHAL STRIKE* because you had the courage to become "Nothing" so that He could be "Everything."

WEEK 1

THE EXCAVATION (Character)

DAY 1: The Audit of the Throne

- **The Raw Word:** *"I saw the Lord sitting on a throne, high and lifted up."* (Isaiah 6:1).

- **The Lethal Strike:** Today, you must identify who is actually sitting on the throne of your organization. Is it the Mission, or is it your need to be "The One"?.

- **The Challenge:** For the next 24 hours, do not use the words "I," "Me," or "My" in any executive meeting. Observe how difficult it is to speak when "Self" is removed from the center.

DAY 2: The Mirror of Tamiym

- **The Raw Word:** *"Walk before Me and be Tamiym (undivided)."* (Genesis 17:1).

- **The Lethal Strike:** Integrity is the lack of "Fractions." Where are you 70% honest? Where are you 90% transparent?

- **The Challenge:** Identify one "Hidden Fact" about your organizational performance or personal health that you have been "polishing" for the Board. Write the unvarnished truth down. You don't have to send it yet—just look at it.

DAY 3: Killing the Filter

- **The Raw Word:** *"Am I now seeking the approval of man, or of God?"* (Galatians 1:10)
- **The Lethal Strike:** Branding is a filter. Identity is a fire. Filters hide flaws; fire purifies them.
- **The Challenge:** Delete one social media post or promotional graphic today that was designed solely to make you "look good" rather than to serve the mission.

DAY 4: The Sound of Silence

- **The Raw Word:** *"But Jesus remained silent."* (Matthew 26:63).

- **The Lethal Strike:** A leader who must always have the "Last Word" is a leader who is terrified of the Vacuum..

- **The Challenge:** In every meeting today, you are permitted to ask questions, but you are forbidden from making statements.
Let the vacuum grow.

DAY 5: The Shadow Scan

- **The Raw Word:** *"Nothing is hidden that will not be revealed."* (Luke 8:17)

- **The Lethal Strike:** Your "Shadow" is the part of your leadership you refuse to acknowledge. If you don't lead your shadow, your shadow will lead you.

- **The Challenge:** Ask a trusted subordinate: *"What is it like to be on the other side of my leadership when I'm stressed?"* Listen. Do not defend.

DAY 6: The Currency of Approval

- **The Raw Word:** *"They loved the glory that comes from man more than the glory that comes from God."* (John 12:43).

- **The Lethal Strike:** What "Currency" are you trading in? Is it the "Likes" of the Crowd or the "Well Done" of the Cloud?

- **The Challenge:** Perform an anonymous act of service for a competitor or a critic today.

DAY 7: The Sabbath of the Sovereign

- **The Raw Word:** *"Be still, and know that I am God."* (Psalm 46:10).

- **The Lethal Strike:** If the organization collapses because you took a day off, you aren't a leader; you're a bottleneck.

- **The Challenge:** Complete digital disconnection for 24 hours. No emails. No "Check-ins." Trust the DNA you've built to hold the floor.

WEEK 2

THE BRAID (Competence)

DAY 8: Identifying the Money Changers

- **The Raw Word:** *"He found in the temple those selling oxen and sheep..."* (John 2:14).

- **The Lethal Strike:** The "Money Changers" aren't always people; sometimes they are legacy programs that charge a "tax" on your team's energy without producing Kingdom fruit.

- **The Challenge:** List every recurring meeting in your organization. Identify the one that is "selling oxen"— consuming time without generating presence. Kill it.

DAY 9: Weaving the Cord

- **The Raw Word:** *"And making a whip of cords..."* (John 2:15)
- **The Lethal Strike:** The "Braid" takes time. Speed is the enemy of surgical discipline.

- **The Challenge:** Identify a conflict you've been avoiding. Spend today "weaving"—gathering data, praying for the person, and aligning your heart. Do not strike today. Just prepare the Braid.

DAY 10: The Precision Strike

The Raw Word: *"He overturned the tables."* (John 2:15)

- **The Lethal Strike:** Notice Jesus didn't break the walls; He flipped the tables. He targeted the *behavior*, not the *structure*.

- **The Challenge:** Execute the "Braid" conversation you prepared yesterday. Target the "Table" (the specific toxic action) with 100% clarity. Leave the person's dignity intact.

WEEK 3

THE TRANSFUSION (Calling)

DAY 11: The Net-Washer's Scout

- **The Raw Word:** *"And He saw two brothers... casting a net into the sea."* (Matthew 4:18)

- **The Lethal Strike:** We often hire for "Presentation," but Jesus hired for "Posture." He looked for those already in motion, even in the mundane.

- **The Challenge:** Today, walk through the "hidden" parts of your organization. Look for someone doing a job they weren't assigned, simply because it needed to be done. This is your next leader.

DAY 12: Selective Intimacy (The 80/20 Rule)

- **The Raw Word:** *"He did not permit anyone to follow Him except Peter, James, and John."* (Mark 5:37).

- **The Lethal Strike:** Accessibility is a myth that kills multiplication. If you are available to everyone, you are deep with no one.

- **The Challenge:** Look at your calendar for the next two weeks. Identify the "Many" who are consuming your time and the "Few" who carry your DNA. Pivot 20% of your "Many" time into "Deep Water" time with your "Three."

DAY 13: The Agrammatos Advantage

* **The Raw Word:** *"Now when they saw the boldness of Peter and John, and perceived that they were uneducated and untrained men, they marveled."* (Acts 4:13)

* **The Lethal Strike:** A "Polished" resume can often hide a hollow spirit. A "Rough" history often produces a resilient soul.

* **The Challenge:** In your next hiring or promotion meeting, ignore the "Degrees" section of the resume. Ask only for the candidate's history of "Net-Washing" and "Wilderness Survival."

DAY 14: Transfusing the "Why"

* **The Raw Word:** *"For I have given you an example, that you should do as I have done to you."* (John 13:15).

* **The Lethal Strike:** Teaching is the transfer of information. Transfusion is the transfer of identity.

* **The Challenge:** Today, do not delegate a task. Delegate a *perspective*. When you give an assignment, spend 10 minutes explaining the **Heart** behind it, not just the **How** of it.

DAY 15: The Gethsemane Grit Test

* **The Raw Word:** *"Stay here and watch with Me."* (Matthew 26:38).

* **The Lethal Strike:** True partners aren't those who celebrate your victories; they are those who can "watch" with you in the dark.

- **The Challenge:** Identify who on your team stayed when things were "Empty." Send them a handwritten note today, acknowledging their **Hupomonē** (endurance).

DAY 16: The Death of the Soloist

- **The Raw Word:** *"Two are better than one... for if they fall, one will lift up his companion."* (Ecclesiastes 4:9-10).

- **The Lethal Strike:** A leader who works alone is a leader who is afraid of being surpassed.

- **The Challenge:** Identify one project you are currently "hoarding." Hand the steering wheel to a subordinate today. Your only job is to sit in the passenger seat and stay silent.

DAY 17: The Sabbath of the Shepherd

- **The Raw Word:** *"The Lord is my shepherd; I shall not want."* (Psalm 23:1).

- **The Lethal Strike:** You cannot transfuse life if you are spiritually dehydrated.

- **The Challenge:** 24 hours of rest. No "Shepherding" allowed. Remind yourself that the Great Shepherd does not need your help to keep the world spinning.

WEEK 4

THE SYMMETRY (The Lion & The Lamb)

DAY 18: The Basin of Authority

- **The Raw Word:** *"He poured water into a basin..."* (John 13:5)

- **The Lethal Strike:** The Basin is the prerequisite for the Scepter.

- **The Challenge:** Clean something today that you usually pay someone else to clean. Do it as a prophetic act of reclaiming your "Servant Identity."

DAY 19: The Lion's Roar (Truth-Telling)

- **The Raw Word:** *"Woe to you, scribes and Pharisees, hypocrites!"* (Matthew 23:13).

- **The Lethal Strike:** A "Lamb" who cannot roar is not a leader; they are an enabler.

- **The Challenge:** Speak a "Hard Truth" today that you have been softening with "Nice" language. Roar for the sake of the mission.

DAY 20: The Lamb's Silence (Under Fire)

- **The Raw Word:** *"He was oppressed and He was afflicted, yet He opened not His mouth."* (Isaiah 53:7).

-

- **The Lethal Strike:** The ultimate power is the power to NOT strike back when you have the means to do so.

- **The Challenge:** If you receive a critical email or a "jab" in a meeting today, do not respond. Let the silence be your "Lethal Strike."

DAY 21: The Surgical Strike (Policy vs. Person)

- **The Raw Word:** *"The Sabbath was made for man, and not man for the Sabbath."* (Mark 2:27)

- **The Lethal Strike:** We often protect the "System" at the expense of the "Soul."

- **The Challenge:** Identify one internal policy that is "Crushing the Lambs." Change it or kill it today.

DAY 22: The Weight of the Glory

- **The Raw Word:** *"For our light affliction... is working for us a far more exceeding and eternal weight of glory."* (2 Corinthians 4:17)
- **The Lethal Strike:** Character is the only thing that makes the "Weight" of leadership sustainable.

- **The Challenge:** Reflect on your heaviest "Affliction" this year. How has it added "Weight" (authority) to your spirit?

DAY 23: The Table of the Disinherited

- **The Raw Word:** *"But when you give a feast, invite the poor, the maimed, the lame, the blind."* (Luke 14:13),

-

- **The Lethal Strike:** A Sovereign Leader does not network up; they network down.

- **The Challenge:** Take someone from the "bottom" of your organizational chart to lunch. Ask them what they see that you don't.

DAY 24: The Sabbath of the Scars

- **The Raw Word:** *"Reach your finger here, and look at My hands."* (John 20:27).

- **The Lethal Strike:** Your scars are your credentials.

- **The Challenge:** Rest and reflect on your "Leadership Scars." Give thanks for the wounds that taught you how to lead.

WEEK 5

THE ARCHITECTURE OF ABSENCE (Commitment)

DAY 25: The Bottleneck Audit

- **The Raw Word:** *"Moses' father-in-law said to him, 'The thing that you do is not good... you will surely wear away.'"* (Exodus 18:17-18)

- **The Post-Mortem Analysis:** A leader who is a "Bottleneck" is often suffering from a misplaced sense of "Stewardship." You believe you are being "thorough," but you are actually being "fearful." If every decision must pass through your desk, you have created an institution that is limited by your personal bandwidth. This is a "Saul" structure.

- **The Lethal Strike:** Identifying the "Points of Friction." Where do people have to wait for you?

- **The Challenge:** Today, identify three approval processes that require your signature. **Abolish them.** Delegate the final authority to the person closest to the problem.

DAY 26: The "It Is Finished" Metric

- **The Raw Word:** *"I have finished the work which You have given Me to do."* (John 17:4)

- **The Post-Mortem Analysis:** "Finished" does not mean you have done everything; it means you have done the **Specific**

Thing you were called to do. Many leaders fail to exit because they keep inventing new "works" to justify their stay.

- **The Lethal Strike:** Distinguishing between "Maintenance" and "Assignment."

- **The Challenge:** Write a list of your current responsibilities. Cross out everything that someone else *could* do, even if they do it 20% worse than you. What is left is your "Assignment." Everything else is a distraction.

DAY 27: The Succession Fast

- **The Raw Word:** *"And He went up on the mountain and called to Him those He Himself wanted."* (Mark 3:13)

- **The Post-Mortem Analysis:** Succession is not a moment; it is a momentum. A "Sovereign Fast" involves fasting from your own importance. You must intentionally "dim your light" so that the light of your successor can be seen.

- **The Lethal Strike:** The "Voluntary Shadow."

- **The Challenge:** In your primary meeting today, do not sit at the head of the table. Sit in a side chair. Let your "Number Two" lead the entire agenda. Do not jump in to "save" them if they stumble. Let them feel the weight of the floor.

DAY 28: The Reputation Funeral

- **The Raw Word:** *"For you died, and your life is hidden with*

- *Christ in God."* (Colossians 3:3).

- **The Post-Mortem Analysis:** You cannot perform a
  "Cruciform Exit" if you are still worried about what people

  will say after you leave. If you are building a legacy for your
  own name, you will never truly hand over the keys.
- **The Lethal Strike:** The "Ego Death" of the Founder.

- **The Challenge:** Write your own "Leadership Obituary" from
  the perspective of the **Cloud of Witnesses**. Focus only on
  your "Nothingness" and the "Fullness" of the Mission you
  left behind.

DAY 29: The Transfer of the Keys

- **The Raw Word:** *"I will give you the keys of the kingdom..."*
  (Matthew 16:19).

- **The Post-Mortem Analysis:** In the Kingdom, "Keys"
  represent the authority to bind and loose—to make
  highstakes decisions. If you hold all the keys, you are a
  jailer, not a leader.
- **The Lethal Strike:** The "Strategic Unlock."

- **The Challenge:** Physically identify one "Key" (a password,
  a credit card, a hiring right) that you have held onto for too
  long. **Hand it over today.** Give the person the "Right to
  Fail" with that key.

DAY 30: The Silence of the Departure

- **The Raw Word:** *"It is to your advantage that I go away."*

  (John 16:7).

- **The Post-Mortem Analysis:** This is the most counterintuitive "Lethal Strike" in the book. Your absence is often more valuable than your presence because absence creates the **Vacuum** that pulls others into their destiny.

- **The Lethal Strike:** The "Advantage of Absence."

- **The Challenge:** Plan a "Departure Drill." For the next 72 hours, you are to be "digitally dead" to your organization. No emergency calls. No check-ins. Observe who rises to the occasion.

DAY 31: The Gideon Strike (Reducing the Army)

- **The Raw Word:** *"The people who are with you are too many... lest Israel claim glory for itself."* (Judges 7:2)

- **The Post-Mortem Analysis:** Sometimes, competence means *reducing* resources to increase reliance on the Spirit. "Fullness" of staff and budget can mask a "Nothingness" of faith.
- **The Lethal Strike:** The "Efficiency of the Few."

- **The Challenge:** Audit your "Army." Where are you relying on "Numbers" (money, staff, tech) rather than the "Raw Word"? Identify one area where you can "cut the army" to increase the "Strike."

DAY 32: The Cloud-Gaze Alignment

- **The Raw Word:** *"Since we are surrounded by so great a cloud of witnesses..."* (Hebrews 12:1).

- **The Post-Mortem Analysis:** This is the final pivot. The "Cloud" doesn't want your success; they want your **Endurance**. They are cheering for the "Sovereign Stay" in the middle of the "Midnight Season."

- **The Lethal Strike:** The "Eschatological Compass."

- **The Challenge:** Spend 30 minutes in total darkness today. Imagine the Cloud of Witnesses looking down at your current struggle. What would Paul say? What would the martyred saints say? Align your next decision with their perspective, not the Board's.

WEEK 6

THE SOVEREIGN FINALE (The Cloud of Witnesses)

DAY 33: The Fast of the Future

- The Raw Word: *"Do not boast about tomorrow, for you do not know what a day may bring forth."* (Proverbs 27:1).

- The Post-Mortem Analysis: Leaders are often addicted to "Future-Gazing" as a way to avoid the "Friction" of the present. We build "Five-Year Plans" to hide from the fact that we aren't "Tamiym" (whole) today. A Sovereign Leader fasts from the anxiety of the future to master the "Lethal Strike" of the *Now*.

- The Lethal Strike: The "Presence Protocol."

- The Challenge: Cancel all "Long-Range Planning" conversations for today. Spend the day addressing the "Elephant in the Room" that you've been ignoring in favor of "Future Vision."

DAY 34: The Weight of the "Well Done"

- The Raw Word: *"His lord said to him, 'Well done, good and faithful servant.'"* (Matthew 25:21).

- The Post-Mortem Analysis: In the economy of the Cloud, "Success" is a carnal metric. "Faithfulness" is the only

currency that converts. Most leaders are "Good" but not
- "Faithful" to the specific, hidden burden they were given.
  They trade their "Burden" for a "Brand."
- The Lethal Strike: The "Audience of One."

- The Challenge: Identify one project that has brought you
  much "Glory" but has cost you your "Peace." Repent of the
  trade. Re-align the project with "Faithfulness" rather than
  "Visibility."

DAY 35: The Hupomonē of the Midnight Season

- The Raw Word: *"But at midnight Paul and Silas were
  praying and singing hymns..."* (Acts 16:25).

- The Post-Mortem Analysis: Midnight is the time when the
  "Crowd" is asleep and only the "Cloud" is watching. Your
  leadership is not defined by your "Morning Speeches" (when
  things are rising), but by your "Midnight Songs" (when you
  are in the stocks).

- The Lethal Strike: The "Prison-Cell Praise."

- The Challenge: Find the area of your organization that feels
  most like a "Prison" right now (financial lack, legal trouble,
  or personnel betrayal). Write a "Hymn of Strategy"—a
  declaration of God's sovereignty over that specific darkness.

DAY 36: The Anatomy of the Scar

- The Raw Word: *"From now on let no one trouble me, for I
  bear in my body the marks of the Lord Jesus."* (Galatians
  6:17).

- The Post-Mortem Analysis: Paul's "Lethal Strike" came from his *Stigmata*—his scars. A leader without scars is a leader who has never been to the front lines. Scars are the

  "Credentials of the Sovereign." They prove you didn't flee when the "Lion" roared.

- The Lethal Strike: The "Vulnerability of the Veteran." • The Challenge: Share the story of your most painful "Leadership Wound" with your inner circle today. Do not share it as a victim, but as a "Sovereign" who survived the Strike.

DAY 37: The Anti-Monument Decree

- The Raw Word: *"Unless the Lord builds the house, they labor in vain who build it."* (Psalm 127:1).

- The Post-Mortem Analysis: We have a biological urge to build "Monuments" (buildings, systems, or legacies with our names on them). But a "Monument" is just a "Tomb" for a past move of God. We are called to build "Movements," which are living organisms that require the leader to "Die" so the Body can live.

- The Lethal Strike: The "Iconoclast Maneuver."

- The Challenge: Look at your organization's physical and digital spaces. Remove one "Monument" to yourself—a photo, a plaque, or a bio that overstates your importance.

DAY 38: The Great Cloud Communion

- The Raw Word: *"And these all... did not receive the promise, God having provided something better for us."* (Hebrews 11:39-40).

- The Post-Mortem Analysis: You are not alone in the "Friction." You are part of a lineage of "Sovereign Nothings." When you feel the weight of the scepter,

  remember that there is a "Cloud" of millions who carried it before you and are waiting for you to finish your lap.

- The Lethal Strike: The "Lineage of the Lamb."

- The Challenge: Read Hebrews 11 aloud in your office. Declare yourself a "Co-Heir" of that same "Grit."

DAY 39: The Final Braid (Agape)

- The Raw Word: *"But above all these things put on love, which is the bond of perfection."* (Colossians 3:14).

- The Post-Mortem Analysis: The final "Cord" in the Braid is not "Authority" or "Competence"—it is Love (*Agape*). If you flip tables without love, you are just a vandal. If you wash feet without love, you are just a politician. Love is the "Lethal Strike" that changes the atmosphere forever.

- The Lethal Strike: The "Agape Audit."

- The Challenge: Identify the person in your organization you like the *least*. Spend today interceding for their success as if it were your own.

DAY 40: The Sovereign Strike (Tetelestai)

- The Raw Word: *"And He bowed His head and gave up His spirit."* (John 19:30).

- The Post-Mortem Analysis: This is the end of the Fast and the beginning of the Mission. You have been emptied. You have been braided. You have been transfused. Now, you must "Give up your spirit"—the spirit of control—and let the King lead through the "Nothing" you have become.

- The Lethal Strike: The "Final Relinquishment."

- The Challenge: Go to your team. Tell them:

"I am not your source. I am not your King. I am your fellow bondservant. Let's go and clear the room."

PART I: FOUNDATIONS & THE ONTOLOGICAL SHIFT

CHAPTER 1: THE VACUUM OF POWER

Theological Thesis: Christian leadership begins with the *Kenosis* (emptying) of the self. To THE LETHAL STRIKE is to create a functional vacuum where the ego once sat, allowing the authority of God to fill the void.

- The Raw Word: *Philippians 2:5-11*. Christ "made Himself nothing." In leadership, "Nothing" is the most dangerous thing you can be because you cannot be toppled, manipulated, or intimidated if you have already surrendered your reputation.

- Executive Friction: The "CEO-Self" seeks to take up more space. The Christ-Leader seeks to create space for others to thrive.

- The Practicum: The "Last Word" Fast. Spend one week yielding the final word in every meeting to a subordinate.

CHAPTER 2:   HOLY FRICTION (THE LAMB WITH A WHIP)

Theological Thesis: Service is not passivity. True Christ-like competence requires the ability to switch between washing feet and flipping tables in the same hour.

- The Raw Word: *John 2:13-17*. Jesus' disruption of the Temple was not an emotional outburst; it was a premeditated, surgical strike.

- The Strike: You must carry the Symmetry of the Scars. Your right to use the "Whip" of correction is earned by your willingness to use the "Towel" of service.

- The Practicum: The Money-Changer Audit. Identify one toxic high-performer in your organization and "Braid the Cord" for a confrontation.

PART II: THE FIRST C – CHARACTER

CHAPTER 3: THE TAMIYM FACTOR (INTEGRITY)

Theological Thesis: Character is the internal architecture that sustains the weight of public authority.

- The Raw Word: *Tamiym* (Wholeness). Integrity is the structural soundness of a leader whose private life is larger than their public platform.

- The Strike: If your visibility grows faster than your hidden character, the platform will eventually crush the person.

- The Practicum: The Solitude Audit. 60 minutes of absolute silence with no devices to see who you are when no one is watching.

CHAPTER 4: KILLING THE IMAGE (CHRIST-IDENTITY)

Theological Thesis: A leader who is obsessed with their "Personal Brand" is a leader who is enslaved to the crowd.

- The Raw Word: *Galatians 2:20*. "I have been crucified with Christ." A dead man has no reputation to defend.

- The Strike: The Reputation Fast. When you are misunderstood or unfairly criticized, choose not to defend yourself. Let God be your Vindicator.

PART III: THE SECOND C – COMPETENCE

CHAPTER 5: THE SYMMETRY OF AUTHORITY

Theological Thesis: Competence is the stewardship of both the Lion's power and the Lamb's sacrifice.

- The Strike: Authority is not about control; it is about Protection. You are the Shepherd who stands between the wolves and the sheep.

- The Practicum: Ask your team: "Do I lean toward being a doormat or a dictator when under pressure?" Balance the score.

CHAPTER 6: BRAIDING THE CORD (STÉWARDSHIP)

Theological Thesis: Competence in the Kingdom is the intentional craftsmanship of your skills to serve the Master.

- The Raw Word: *Poiēma* (Workmanship). You are God's "handiwork" designed for "good works."

- The Strike: Stop "winging it" on anointing. Study your craft. Become world-class so the world cannot ignore your message.

PART IV: THE THIRD C – CALLING

CHAPTER 7: DISCERNING DIVINE PURPOSE

Theological Thesis: Calling is a sovereign assignment that provides both the fuel and the boundaries for your life.

- The Strike: Career is what you do for yourself; Calling is what you do for the Master. One ends in retirement; the other ends in "It is Finished."

CHAPTER 8: THE RECRUITMENT PARADOX (THE TWELVE)

Theological Thesis: God bypasses the "Elite" to find the "Available."

- The Raw Word: *Agrammatos* (Unlettered). Why Jesus chose fishermen over Pharisees.

- The Strike: Hire for Callouses over Credentials. Look for those who have a history of hidden faithfulness.

PART V: THE FOURTH C – COMMITMENT & LEGACY

CHAPTER 9: TESTING AND THE GETHSEMANE GRIT

Theological Thesis: Commitment is revealed in the garden, not on the mountaintop.

- The Strike: Endurance is the "Lethal Strike" against the enemy. If you stay when it is hard, you win.

CHAPTER 10: THE CRUCIFORM EXIT

Theological Thesis: The ultimate goal of leadership is to become obsolete.

- The Raw Word: *Tetelestai* (It is Finished).

- The Strike: Success is measured by how the mission functions when you are gone. If the organization dies when you leave, you were a King, not a Christ-leader.

- The Practicum: The Succession Audit. Hand over one "Key" of authority to a subordinate this week.

THE APPENDICES (RE-COMPILED)

1. Appendix A: The 12-Week Syllabus (Institutional Syllabus).

2. Appendix B: The Formation Rubric (Lion vs. Lamb Grading).

3. The Executive Summary: The 4 Cs Cheat Sheet.

THE PROPHETIC VOICE BEHIND THE STRIKE

Laeticia is a voice calling from the intersection of **Marketplace Strategy** and **Spiritual Formation**. A "Net-Washer" by trade and a "Sovereign Servant" by calling, she has spent years navigating the "Friction" between institutional success and Kingdom integrity. Her work is defined by the **"Lethal Strike"**—the conviction that true leadership only begins when the leader's own ambition has been surrendered to the **Cloud of Witnesses**. Having navigated the corridors of high-stakes executive leadership and the "Hidden Years" of deep-water ministry, Laeticia writes not from a place of theoretical polish, but from the "Callouses" of experience.

She is a strategist for the "Nobodies," a mentor to the "Agrammatos," and a disruptor of the "Saul Regime." Her mission is to see a new generation of leaders rise who can **"Wash Feet and Braid Cords"** with equal spiritual intensity—leaders who are unbuyable, un-cancelable, and un-wavering in their pursuit of the King's Presence.

Through her writing, coaching, and strategic consulting, Laeticia continues to advocate for the **Cruciform Exit**, challenging founders and executives to build legacies that outlive their names and missions that reflect the **Symmetry of the Lion and the Lamb**. She lives and leads under the radical realization that she is a **Sovereign Nothing**, devoted to the "Somebody" named Jesus.

GLOSSARY OF SOVEREIGN TERMS

The Vocabulary of the Strike

Agrammatos (Gr. ἀγράμματος)

Literally, "unlettered" or "without formal credentials." In the Sovereign Strike framework, this refers to a leader whose authority is derived from *Selective Intimacy* with Christ rather than institutional validation. It is the "Advantage of the Nobody" (See Chapter 3).

Arche (Gr. ἀρχή):
The right to rule; beginning; origin. The world leads from the *Arche* (positional power). The Sovereign Leader voluntarily vacates their *Arche* to enter into the *Kenosis Protocol*.

The Braid:

A premeditated executive discipline. It represents the "Quiet Preparation" of a leader before a "Public Strike." It is the fusion of the Lamb's patience and the Lion's precision (See Chapter 7).

The Cloud of Witnesses (Gr. νέφος μαρτύρων):

The multi-generational assembly of saints (Hebrews 12:1) who serve as the Sovereign Leader's primary audience. To lead for the "Cloud" is to be liberated from the "Idol of the Audience" (the Crowd).

Cruciform Exit:

The strategic and theological process of designing one's own obsolescence. It is the "It Is Finished" moment where a leader successfully hands the baton to a successor, ensuring the mission outlives the man.

Doulos (Gr. δοῦλος):

A bondservant or slave by choice. The *Doulos* is the identity of a leader who has no reputation to protect and no rights to defend. This "Nothingness" is the source of the leader's lethal speed.

Fullness vs. Nothingness:

The primary tension of the book. "Fullness" refers to the Saul Regime—leading from resources, ego, and visibility. "Nothingness" refers to the Davidic model—leading from the Vacuum created by self-emptying (Kenosis).

Grit Perception:

The executive skill of identifying *Hupomonē* in potential recruits. It is the ability to see past a polished resume to find the "Callouses" of a true worker.

Hupomonē (Gr. ὑπομονή):

Endurance; the power to remain under a heavy weight without breaking. It is the defining characteristic of a "Net-Washer" and the prerequisite for the Sovereign Strike.

Kabod (Heb. כָּבוֹד):

The "Weight of Glory." In leadership, the *Kabod* is the manifest presence of God that rests on an organization. Only a leader with *Tamiym* (wholeness) can support the weight of the *Kabod* without collapsing.

Kenosis (Gr. κένωσις):

The act of self-emptying. As Christ emptied Himself (Philippians 2:7), the Sovereign Leader empties themselves of ambition and image to create a vacuum for the Spirit to fill.

Lethal Strike:

The surgical application of truth and authority that clears the room of toxicity. It is never carnal; it is always surgical, targeting the "System" or the "Money Changer" rather than the soul.

Money Changers:

Institutional gatekeepers who charge a "tax" on the Presence of God. They represent the paywalls, the ego-driven policies, and the transactional cultures that the Sovereign Leader must flip.

Net-Washing:

The unglamorous, repetitive, and hidden work of leadership preparation. It is the "Hidden Years" where a leader's character is forged before they are given the "Strike."

Symmetry (Lion-Lamb):

The perfect fusion of two seemingly opposite natures. The Lamb (The Basin/The Towel) and the Lion (The Whip/The Roar). To lead with symmetry is to be tender to the broken and lethal to the proud.

Tamiym (Heb. תָּמִים):

Wholeness; undividedness; integrity. It is the "Architecture of the Soul" that ensures there is no gap between the leader's public platform and private closet.

1. The Seminary Discussion Guide (The "Must Read" Factor

Seminary Discussion & Cohort Guide

1. The Seminary Discussion Guide (The "Must-Read" Factor)

This section is designed for immediate use in leadership meetings or classroom settings to challenge the foundational motives of the leader.

- **On Kenosis (Self-Emptying)**

- **Question:** In your current role, what "space" are you filling that should be left as a vacuum for others (or for God) to occupy?

- **Objective:** To identify where your "competence" has become a "crutch" that prevents others from growing.

- **On the Braid (Premeditated Discipline)**

- **Question:** When was the last time you "braided a cord" (premeditated discipline) versus reacting out of carnal frustration?

- **Objective:** To distinguish between righteous zeal (which is prepared) and unbridled anger (which is reactive).

ABOUT THE AUTHOR

Laeticia Amaka Anene** is a voice calling for a radical reconstruction of power. Operating at the intersection of executive strategy and spiritual formation, she has spent her career deconstructing the "Saul Regime" to make room for the "Sovereign Strike" of Christ-centered leadership.

A practitioner who values **callouses over credentials**, Laeticia's leadership was fire-tested in the trenches. For decades, she has overseen three global ministries, conducted healing conferences, and managed free medical missions across East and West Africa.

Known for her **"Lion-Lamb Symmetry,"** her work is dedicated to the "Sovereign Nothings"—leaders ready to trade their personal brand for a Divine mandate. When she isn't "braiding cords" or "washing feet," she is equipping a new generation of reformers to lead for the **Cloud of Witnesses** rather than the crowd of the present.

THE LETHAL STRIKE

Dismantle the regime.

Embrace the nothing.

Lead the strike.

Leadership in the modern era is often a search for a platform, a pursuit of a brand, and a desperate grab for the *Arche*—the right to rule. But the Kingdom of God operates on a different frequency. It is a frequency of self-emptying, of holy friction, and of the "Lethal Strike" against the ego.

In these pages, Laeticia Amaka Anene issues a summons to the "Sovereign Nothings." This is not a manual for management; it is a manifesto for the crucified life. It is for the leader who is tired of the Saul Regime and ready for the Gethsemane Grit. It is for those who realize that the only way to truly lead is to first be struck down by the King.

The Work is Finished. The blade is sharpened. The vacuum is waiting.

Will you occupy the space, or will you occupy the Cloud